ISBN 978-1-5276-8728-8
PIBN 10218602

1 MONTH OF
FREE
READING

at

www.ForgottenBooks.com

By purchasing this book you are eligible for one month membership to ForgottenBooks.com, giving you unlimited access to our entire collection of over 1,000,000 titles via our web site and mobile apps.

To claim your free month visit:

www.forgottenbooks.com/free218602

THE

CONFLICT OF GOOD AND EVIL

IN OUR DAY.

TWELVE LETTERS TO A MISSIONARY.

BY THE REV. F. D. MAURICE, M.A.,

INCUMBENT OF ST. P. TER'S, MARYLEBONE

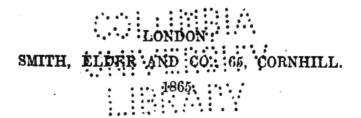

LONDON:
SMITH, ELDER AND CO. 65, CORNHILL.
1865.

CONTENTS.

LETTER   PAGE

   I. THE BISHOP'S WARNINGS.. 1

  II. THE CHOLERA, AND DISEASES IN GENERAL 12

 III. THE SALVATION OF THE SOUL..................................... 25

 IV. FREE-THINKING.. 36

  V. FREEDOM OF CONSCIENCE.. 45

 VI. FREEDOM OF THE WILL 56

VII. CONVERSION 70

VIII. CHRIST AND ANTICHRIST 90

 IX. HERESIES AND PERSECUTIONS 120

  X. SACRIFICES TO GOD AND TO THE EVIL SPIRIT 152

 XI. THE CHURCH OF THE ETERNAL 177

XII. CHRISTIANITY AND CIVILIZATION 198

PREFACE.

The speech of the Lord Bishop of Oxford, to which I have alluded so often in these letters, was delivered at a meeting of the two Societies for the Propagation of the Gospel, and for the Promotion of Christian Knowledge, in Salisbury. A report will be found in the *Guardian* of August 23rd. From that paper I extract the passages on which I have commented.

I.

"I have no doubt myself that the last attempt upon the faith of Christ will come, not with an open denial of its verity, but with a courteous admission of its truth. At the same time there will be a sapping of its distinctive features."

II.

"I have no doubt myself that unbelief contains within itself the seed of the most intensely hating persecution which the world has ever seen.

Instead of being tolerant, I believe it is the very perfection of intolerance. I believe when it has achieved its own victory, toleration will be the thing which above all others it will hate with an intensity short only of the hatred which the Evil Spirit has for the simple gospel of the Lord Jesus Christ.

III.

"It must be so, I think, because unbelief, in whatever form it comes, is the exaltation of the human intellect and human will over the voice of revelation and revealed knowledge. It is thwarted to the utmost the very moment it is confronted by the mighty rock of revealed Truth. The stream flows on with the most delicious smoothness when there is nothing to thwart it. 'Let us love one another, let us be tolerant of one another's views. If you choose to worship the devil, worship him, if you only do it quietly: if you choose to worship an Anti-devil, so do, if you only do it quietly; let us go on altogether in our worldly ways and worldly thoughts, holding nothing that may be troublesome or disagreeable. Anything disagreeable in religion is such a shocking thing.' Well, then comes the most disagreeable thing possible, which says, 'We have nothing to do with this fellowship of Evil. You are leading men to absolute destruction. You are promising them liberty, and making them slaves. You are handing them over to the devil under the pretence of emancipation from their shackles.' (Applause.) And forthwith these men turn upon the stern declaration of the eternal verity of God with all the hatred of the human heart which the great rebel himself can stir up within it."

IV.

" Believing, then, as I do, that there may be heard upon the winds these footfalls of the coming of the great Antichrist; that this which we hear whispered, and spreading, we know not how, through the air, is just the precursing atmosphere which comes before his advent—I say it is the time, if ever the time was, for those who fear and love the Lord, to be rousing themselves up and to be working mightily that they may establish indeed the hiding-places of the faith throughout the earth. . . . . And how is this to be obtained? Most directly and immediately, I believe, by great missionary efforts."

V.

" Who can doubt that it is so? When we read only to-day in the cathedral of God, ' *I will send great plagues upon men and beasts,'* could any of you help thinking of the signs of the present time? Is not this mysterious disease which has entered among our cattle at this moment—is not that, if the Bible be true, one of God's handwritings on the nation's wall, warning them to turn to Him? .... Then remember the whisper rising now almost into a voice, of the onward march of the old pestilence of the cholera, which I remember so well in this city, at its great visitation. It is again rustling upon the breeze of the evening. And is not this another of God's writings on the wall, warning you that you do His work, and turn to Him while yet the opportunity of turning to Him is left?"

These are the sentences of the speech which chiefly concern my subject. I have alluded to some others, which contained an attack upon the Bishop of Natal. I omit them as much from respect to the accuser as to the accused.

I ought to say that the person to whom these letters are addressed, will not see them till they reach him in this volume.

THE CONFLICT

OF

GOOD AND EVIL IN OUR DAY.

LETTER I.

THE BISHOP'S WARNINGS.

MY DEAR FRIEND,—Why have I not done more to strengthen you in your hard conflict with heathens and Mahometans, to cheer you in your separation from the blessings of Christendom? You may well ask me this question. I have asked it myself very often. The answers which my conscience has heard may console you for my silence; but they testify against my coldness and infidelity.

I could not strengthen you in your conflict, for I was full of despondency about it myself.

1

"What are our missionaries doing?" is a demand which we hear continually. "Those reports which we read, those speeches which are made at their public meetings, tell us nothing. We cannot trust them. The most faithful narratives we can get are narratives of failure and disappointment. The converts, how few they are! Are those few the salt which can penetrate the surrounding mass and purify it? Where are the signs of any great movement like that which moulded the European nations into a Christendom? The colonists are energetic and able, full of zeal and enterprise. But what do they care for the conversion of the natives to Christianity? How many of them believe in it? Are not all our religious debates repeated with even increased fury amongst those who go forth to preach of one Lord, one faith, one baptism? Missionaries talk about the bad morals of civilians and military men. Are not these strifes amongst themselves more fatal to their work, and more direct confutations of their arguments?" Whilst such words were ringing in my ears, and exercising, I will not deny it, a great influence over my heart and mind, what could I say which might not add to the thousand perplexities by which you are beset?

And then as to your isolation from Christendom. Ah, my friend! how often those who live in the midst of it are tempted to reckon that among your advantages! That it is most ungrateful to do so,—that we should feel the tremendous difference, if the atmosphere by which we are surrounded were exchanged for yours,—this in our hearts we know very well. We are not quite young enough to dream of any beauty in savage existence; Oriental civilization can scarcely fascinate any who are not dreamers; any serious men who understand what it is. But you know what confessions we make of our state, even while we boast that we are better than all the nations of the West. The confessions certainly fall below the truth, whatever may be the truth of the boast. Is it not difficult, then, to pretend that we count our position an enviable one, or that we sincerely deplore the lot of those who have left it behind them?

Then though a number of answers, clever and even satisfactory in their way, have been made to the cry so often raised in the newspapers, "What! ask for help to convert distant lands, when all these wretched multitudes are lying at your doors?"— though *the* answer, that we *do* think it worth while for some purposes to visit distant lands, and to

1—2

settle in them, and that wherever we go or settle we must exercise an influence—for good or for evil—is a sufficient one for all practical purposes; yet the argument appeals to something in us against which reasoning cannot always prevail. If our first business is to renovate those for whom the Bishop of London pleads by his fund, or the crowds which fill our manufacturing towns—even our agricultural labourers—when will there be leisure for the work which is to follow that? When indeed!

My friend, if I was to inflict upon you all these murmurings, was it not better to hold my peace? And yet to write what was not in my mind, or to hide what was, or to speak to you only of domestic interests, would have been a greater wrong. What I have to confess is, not so much my silence as that which caused it: the secret heartlessness and cowardice which unfitted me for holding converse with you—a heartlessness and cowardice as fatal to sincere efforts for the cure of our diseases at home as to any counsels we may offer to you who are afar off.

I can speak, or rather I must speak, to you now, because I have been brought to the conviction that the same causes which make you weak are making us weak; that our dangers are the same; that in spite of the great differences in our circumstances our battle is essentially the same. I have been brought, I say, to this *conviction*: I may have had a general *impression* that it was so, that it could not be otherwise; I may even at times have tried to communicate that impression to my neighbours. But it has been too feeble to resist all the influences of doubt and despondency—all the plausible excuses for indifference—which it encountered. Now those very influences, those plausible excuses appear to me the strongest reasons for claiming fellowship in your labours. The faith and zeal which are deserting us, you may help to rekindle. Instead of our communicating to you, or you to us, the palsy which has benumbed the limbs of both, we may, in God's name, bid each other rise up and walk.

I never expected that the report of words spoken at a missionary meeting would have awakened—have even helped to awaken—this hope in me. The rhetoric at those meetings has done much to weaken my interest, and, I fear, that of many more, in the cause which it professes to uphold. There is something in it against which the sense of truth in our minds vehemently revolts. And yet an address emi-

nently rhetorical—to me most painfully rhetorical—has done me a service, for which I trust
I shall ever be grateful.

In a speech which was delivered by the
Bishop of Oxford last August, he is reported
to have commented on the habit of indifference
to great theological distinctions which is prevalent amongst us.   He said that we might
come at last to confound the worship of God
with the worship of the Devil, and to feel
that it signified nothing which we worshipped.   He said that he saw signs of an approaching manifestation of the Antichrist.   He
warned his hearers that they might become the
servants of the Antichrist, instead of the true
Christ.   He said that when the Antichristian
power was developed, it would be found to be a
persecuting power ; that all our boasted toleration
would then disappear.   He made these his great
pleas for strenuous exertion at home as well as
abroad.

If these statements are true, the inference
from them seems to me inevitable.   The battle
at home, as much as abroad, is with false gods.
We, as much as you, are to turn men from
the worship of tyrants to the worship of a
Deliverer.   And you can give us hints which we

greatly want; you can untie or cut knots for us which are becoming every day more complicated. But are the statements true? Their effect upon devout and earnest minds was much impaired by some sentences which were mixed with them. They took the form of an attack upon a Bishop who was not present to answer for himself, who was charged with undermining the Word of God, and whose arguments were to be met with a shout of indignation. Flowers of rhetoric, which must appear to readers, if not to hearers, artificial and tawdry, were scattered over admonitions, which demanded, if any ever did, simplicity and sternness, an abstinence from anything which had the air of display and trifling. Allusions to the Cholera and the Cattle Plague, blended with language concerning Antichrist, gave that language a sensational, even a grotesque character. Some excellent persons, who read the report of the speech, turned from it, I observed, with disgust, as from a message in which there was a semblance of awe, an absence of reality.

I understood the feeling, and was at first inclined to share in it. But the more I reflected on the substance of the discourse, the more I was convinced that it was both real and awful. I read an able answer to it. The objector com-

plained of the Bishop for misrepresenting the
character of our time, the conflict in which we
are engaged. Good and evil, he said, instead
of standing glaringly apart from each other, as
they did in the time of St. Paul, are strangely
and cunningly interwoven. The skill required of
us is to disentangle the threads. No remarks
can be more true ; none seem more to confirm
the Bishop's warnings. It is precisely the confusion of good and evil which he points out as our
peril. He says, as his critic says, that we are
always hovering between the right and the wrong,
the false and the true, till we forget that there is
any radical difference between them, till one slides
into the other. He thinks such uncertainty
about eternal principles is not to last ; that if
God is what we confess Him to be, it must come
to an end. He holds that if we have that amazing difficulty in discerning between forms which
are everlastingly opposed to each other,—if
we are inclined to deny that they *are* really
opposed—the contrast will in some tremendous
way be made manifest. The more, therefore, he
discovers of that twilight which leads his commentator to discredit the approach of any deci-
sive day that shall scatter the darkness, the more
the Bishop is convinced that such a day must

be at hand. If the premises of the one are right,
I hope the conclusion of the other is right. The
belief that it is right grows more strong in me
the more I look at the signs of our time.

Nor, grievously as I lament the party tone
which the Bishop of Oxford was tempted to give
to warnings that must be needful for all if they
are needful for any, can I deny that they have
an application—a very direct application—to the
controversies which have been recently stirred
respecting the Old Testament. Though the
battle between the God of perfect Truth and
Goodness and the Spirit of Evil may have been
only brought to its complete development when
Christ went into the wilderness to be tempted,—
it is the most obvious, and at the same time the
most profound conception of the Hebrew Scriptures, that they exhibit the conflict between the
true God and false gods. We shall recover that
conception of them, if we learn that the calling of
the chosen people is our calling ; then questions
about the dates of books or the writers of them,
even about the times when the names Elohim
and Jehovah were used or were not used, will not
torment us much or withdraw us from the actual
history. We shall not easily forget in such
arguments a conflict in which all ages and all

classes of men are involved. The critics may carry on their controversy, they will not persuade us that it is the human controversy. And if this return to a more ancient and serious apprehension of the object of these books lowers the exaggerated pretensions of those who discuss their origin, it must also discourage any panic which such discussions have provoked. The Bishop's admonitions, then, are not really, though they may be on the surface, party admonitions. He must have intended, not to direct a shout against certain persons or a certain school, but to say to every man of every school, in a voice which should reach his conscience, " Thou art in danger of worshipping the Devil instead of God. Thou art in danger of exalting the Antichrist into the place of the Christ."

I feel and confess this danger for myself. I began with explaining to you how the want of a full, clear sense of it—which made it greater— has tended to weaken my sympathies with your labours. I wish, if I may be permitted, to write you something which shall be an acknowledgment of that offence, perhaps a slight reparation for it. The words of the Bishop will be the text of all my observations.

At first I was inclined wholly to pass over

his reference to the disease which may invade our land. How much that reference grated upon the moral sense even more than upon the taste of readers whom the Bishop would not have desired to offend, I have hinted. Nevertheless, I have remembered how likely words coming from such a source are to give the key-note to much of the preaching in our pulpits respecting the Cholera, while it is expected and if it should come. I have remembered, also, how much your experience as to the way in which such visitations are regarded by heathens may benefit us. The subject is connected—directly connected —with the question of devil-worship which the Bishop has raised, and which I am anxious to consider. Perhaps it may suggest the simplest illustration of one aspect of that worship. I shall therefore address myself to it in the next letter. —Yours, &c.

LETTER II.

THE CHOLERA, AND DISEASES IN GENERAL.

MY DEAR FRIEND,—You must have been in England during more than one of our visitations of Cholera. With your medical knowledge and medical experience you must have felt painfully the use which was made of it in some of our pulpits. Perhaps your mind will often have been exercised with the question, "In what way should I bring it before my congregation? If I increase the panic, I am doing my best that those who are attacked by the disease should sink under it; that those who are not attacked by it should avoid their neighbours. My preaching, so far as it is of this character, must defeat all the efforts which I or any others may make for the cure of the plague. I shall convince the doctor that his object and ours are not merely different, but opposed. I shall enfeeble the charity which my office as a clergyman binds me to cultivate. Yet what am I to do? Is not this a call to men to repent and to be converted? Am I not to tell them that it is? Am not I separating myself from the teachings of the old Prophets if I say that famines and pestilences are not divine messages to a nation?"

I do not know whether you found any satisfactory answer to these questions. I know you will have done the duty which lay before you; that you will have let no speculations interfere with that. So you will have come at a practical solution of the difficulties, which was better than any theoretical one could be. You will have been sure that you were right in trying to arrest the disorder, and to cheer men whom it assailed. You will have hoped that you should be kept from any wrong mode of speaking about it in church.

Am I mistaken in thinking that your experience in other lands has led you to a much clearer apprehension of the whole subject; to a much more complete reconciliation of your convictions as a physician, and your convictions as a divine; to a far better understanding of the words of the Jewish Prophets? Shall I misrepresent the case if I add that the heathens have taught you these lessons; that they have shown how

.many of the confusions which are working in
their minds were working in your own; what must
be the help against these confusions for them
and for you ?   What they think of diseases, you
had been told before you went among them. You
had heard that they traced every sickness to some
malignant power; that they supposed that power
must be conciliated by some gift or offering before
the disease could be taken away. The commonest
classical reading made you aware of this fact;
you had divested it of all graceful classical asso-
ciations by studying it afresh in the records of
coarse modern idolatry.   No doubt you had
thought with yourself often how greatly medical
knowledge might contribute to the overthrow of
this superstition, how much it might prepare the
way for the Gospel which you were to preach.
But all such anticipations, I should conjecture,
however strengthened by reading and reflection,
prepared you very little for what you were actually
to witness: for the enormous hold which this
feeling—this belief—had on the minds of those
whom you were to teach.   You will sometimes, I should suppose, have said to yourself,
" Surely *this is* the religion of the people ; all
their other religion is merely the outgrowth of
this ; something grafted on the conviction that

disease and death are the messengers of an evil
power." Then you will have altered that opinion.
You will have perceived that there was a faith
fighting in them with this, the acknowledgment
of invisible protectors, powers of life.   You will
have perceived that they turned to the physician,
in whatever form he presented himself, as the
agent of these benevolent powers, the combatant
of the destructive powers. Such observations will
have strengthened your conviction that the art
of medicine must be one of the missionary's main
instruments. You will have begun at once to
work that instrument, to show the poor native
what the knowledge and the tenderness of the
white man could do for him.

  But then to connect this healing with your
preaching; to prove that it was not the white
man, but the white man's GOD from Whom this
knowledge and tenderness proceeded; how was
this to be accomplished ?   Let me ask you to
tell me frankly.   Have not thoughts of this kind
sometimes taken strong possession of your mind ?

  "If I had the miraculous powers which the
Romish missionaries have claimed, and to the
reputation for which they seem to owe much of
their influence, would not the difference between
the dark gods and the white man's God be far

more conspicuous? Could I not then call on the
natives to see that He is a Deliverer, and not a
Destroyer?" Yes! there will have been moments
in which these suggestions will have been vividly
presented to you, in which they will have taken
the form of a temptation. And if as a temptation you treated them—if as a temptation you
overcame them—I am certain you will have found
by degrees a blessed reward. You will have felt
that you were in very deed serving a God of Truth,
Who would be served by no lie; that the conflict in which you were engaged was the conflict
between the Spirit of Truth and the Spirit of Lies.
That grand theological distinction, which is at the
root of all others—and which the Bishop of Oxford
so solemnly and earnestly admonishes us that we
are in peril of losing—will have come out in its
full force before you. The sense of fighting under
such a banner, for such a cause, will have given
you a strength which nothing else could give.

But this blessing will bring another after it.
You wish to show the natives that your God is
a Deliverer, not a Destroyer. Do you want to
make Him out a God of falsehood, that you may
do that? Were you not taught the lesson in
Protestant lands, out of the book to which Protestants and Romanists both appeal? If you

accept the preface to the Ten Commandments, must you not believe that God revealed Himself to the mixed multitude who came out of Egypt, as a Deliverer; that He said they should have no other gods but Him? Is not the whole after history a record of that which came to the Israelites when they set up gods who were not deliverers, in place of Him? Some people say that that history is not authentic. If you and I take it to be authentic, we ought to act as if it were. Then we must hold that the people of Israel fell continually into slavery because they forsook the Deliverer, because they worshipped things in heaven and earth, and ascribed to them the passions of tyrants and slave-makers, or slave-holders. And if we take the Prophets to be inspired teachers, we must suppose that every plague and pestilence which visited their land was a call to turn from the slave-making, slave-holding, destroying gods, to the Deliverer, the God of salvation: a call to put their trust in Him whom they had ceased to trust. That is the broad, simple language which they addressed, not to a portion of the people, but to the whole of them; not to the good, but to the evil. The sin of one and all was distrust in the true God, the righteous God, the God of salvation—was the

2

acknowledgment of false gods, unrighteous gods, gods of damnation. The pestilence came to a self-indulgent, slavish, cowardly people. Their impulse was to bow before it as a dread fate, or else to try if it was not possible to propitiate the tyrant who had taken vengeance for some slight to his altars, some contempt to his priests. Against such propitiations, against all such calculations, the Prophets lifted up their voices. It was the religion which the God of righteousness hated; it was the religion from which He called His people to turn away. He called on them to abandon their refuges of lies, and trust in Him, the God of Truth; to desert the service of death for the service of the Author and Preserver of life, the Enemy of death.

Yes! the Enemy of Death. If we accept the language of the Old Testament literally—if we do not explain it away to suit our rationalizing fancies—we must regard the words of Hosea, which we read in Passion Week, as expressing the Divine purpose: "*I will be thy plague, O death; O grave, I will be thy torment.*" We must read the whole Bible as the record of the fulfilment of this purpose; as the warfare of the Creator with the Destroyer, of Life with Death. The instincts of men in all countries have recognized such a warfare; only the recognition has been imperfect and confused. Manichæism has mingled with it. The Destroyer has been partly a Creator; a portion of the living universe must be referred to him. Once give him a portion, and to all intents and purposes you confess him as supreme. Death is the palpable ruler; all appear to be his servants. If you cannot defy him and utterly deny his rights, his dominion will be regarded as the highest; only certain feeble, insecure privileges will be reserved for the protectors of life. Such is the unbelief—what we call the superstition—of the heathen world: taking very various forms; more fixed and radical in some places and ages than in others—nowhere without striking and mighty witnesses against it.

Your call and office is to bring *the* witness which sustains and interprets all these—which shows how true they are and how weak they are —which declares once for all that Life and Death have tried their strength against each other, and that Life has prevailed. If you have courage to bear that witness as a divine—if it comes clear and full from your lips—all your work as a physician will corroborate it. The more resolutely you strive against plague and pestilence, the more you testify, not for the God

2—2

of the whites, of the Franks, or of Englishmen, but for the God of the whole earth ; the more effectually you can represent every plague and pestilence as a call to cast away the god of death, the destroyer, and to trust in Him. Then there will be no *arrière pensée* towards Jesuit or mediæval miracles, no wish that you could imitate them. You will perceive that they were *not* witnesses for the God of life, only witnesses for a God of power, who could set aside His laws for the purpose of proving certain men to be His servants. If the power of destruction is more startling to men's senses than the power of life, the miracle worker will exercise that. Very commonly it *will* be more startling. To curse, will strike the poor idolater as more like the Divine agency which he expected, than to bless. At all events, the blessing will be capricious, irregular ; the sign of a changeable God, not of a permanent, eternal God. It will be, therefore, no sign of such a God as the Bible speaks of ; rather of such as it denounces.

But if your acts as a physician, and your words as a divine, have that correspondence with each other which I have supposed—then, though you feign to work no miracles as a proof that you can disturb the order of God's universe, you have all

those acts of Christ which we call miracles as tokens
of what that order is.   You will be able to appeal
to His healing of the palsied man, of the deaf,
of the blind, as the Son's discovery, in His
own works, of the works and will of the Father
who sent Him.   You will speak of them as examples in a few cases of what He is doing every
day and hour for the restoration of health, for
the preservation of life ; of what He will do when
He shall have put all enemies under His feet.
The power of His resurrection will therefore be as
substantive and practical a part of your preaching as it was of St. Paul's.   You will argue
about it as little as he did.   You will proclaim
it as a gospel to those who have been all their
lifetime in bondage to the fear of death, that he
who has the power of death—that is, the Devil—
has been vanquished.

You will return—you have returned I doubt
not—to this mode of speaking, to this literal
acceptance of the Divine record, not heeding or
fearing those who may laugh at you for adopting
an old fiction about the Devil; seeing that you
know, from what you see and from what you feel,
from the experience of heathens and your own,
that it is not a fiction; that there is a spirit who is
a murderer and a liar ; that he would lead you as

well as them captive at his will. You are not afraid to speak so, for any fault that your scientific friends may find with you; for you know that you are on their side, whether they think so or not. It is the worship of the spirit of lies which hinders men from recognizing facts of one kind or another; from desiring to understand the truth about any law of Nature, about any of the relations in which human beings stand to each other. Men of science groan under the opposition of this spirit. But they have no arms wherewith to contend against him; they try to grin at him, and he grins much more securely at them. In the name of the eternal God, in the name of the Son of God, who died and rose again from the dead, you can mock him in his high places; you can invite your heathen brethren to arise and cast off his fetters, to take their places as men, as sons of God; not to fear sickness, but by all the wisdom which the God of life imparts, to labour for health; not to fear death, but to cleave mightily to Him who has died and been buried and descended into hell, and has risen again the third day.

And now am I wrong in saying, even if I had not a Bishop's authority for the assertion, that we may learn our duty from you, that you can show us what our perils are, that you can help to

convert us at home as well as the idolaters who
are about you ?   The principle which the Bishop
has laid down is one of the widest application.
At present I would only apply it to the subject
which is pressing on us at this moment, to the
one which was prominent in his speech.   If the
Cholera should come, shall we again fall into an
utter contradiction between our Sunday and
our week-day habits of thinking and acting ?
Shall it be the office of the priest to awaken
terrors which it is the office of the physician to
allay ?   Shall the first imitate his predecessors
who offered incense to Baal, and taught the
people to tremble before an unknown power
which may torment them for their crimes ?   Shall
it be left to the second to imitate the Jewish
Prophet, and say, " Trust, for the power of life
is meant to vanquish the power of death ?"
Shall not the preacher of Christ's Gospel call men
everywhere, pharisees and publicans, saints and
harlots, to repent of having distrusted God, and
of having reverenced the Evil Spirit as being
stronger than He ?   Shall we pretend that we
think disease and death very pretty and pleasant,
when we know that we hate them, and that
every one does hate, and ought to hate them ?
Shall we not say, " They are hateful to us ;

they are hateful to God.   But they may be
turned into His ministers, if they drive us to seek
Him and believe in Him, and utterly to renounce
the service and faith of His enemy.   He is Lord
of all; they are obliged to work for Him.
The Spirit of Lies is compelled to see his own
vassals desert him.   Plagues and pestilences
lead to moral effort, to physical purification.
Terrible wars punish money-worship, and extin-
guish slavery. ·Verily, the Lord God omnipotent
reigneth.   Satan shall be bruised under Christ's
feet."—I am faithfully yours, &c.

LETTER III.

THE SALVATION OF THE SOUL.

MY DEAR FRIEND,—Startling as the assertion of the Bishop of Oxford was, that we in Christian England have reached such a state of theological confusion, that we may at last come to worship the Evil Spirit instead of God, I contended that his language was not exaggerated; that every one of us had need to reflect deeply and earnestly upon it, and to ask himself where the danger lies, how he may escape it, how he may help his brethren to escape it. You, I thought, were reminded directly of that conflict which we are wont to forget, or to describe by specious names very unfaithfully representing its nature. You know that you are failing altogether, unless you can raise men from the worship of dark powers, unless you can bring them to believe in a God of light in whom is no darkness at all. You, therefore, may be our best instructors at this time.

If we can in any degree strengthen your hands, you may much more effectually clear our minds respecting the meaning of the message with which we are entrusted, of the foe which we must encounter.

I have given you one instance of our perplexities, and of the way in which you may show us the way out of them. The question of bodily health and disease, which is forcing itself upon us practically at every moment, demands a theological, as well as a medical treatment. What is that treatment? How are we to speak of the plagues which come near our dwellings? Are we to use them as arguments of terror, or as arguments for trust? You would answer, "If we are to bear witness for the faith of Christendom against the devil-worship of the heathen world, we dare not use them as arguments for fear, we are bound to use them as arguments for trust. We must declare that the God whom we serve is the God of health, the Enemy of sickness and death." It is the broadest and most obvious illustration of the great doctrine which the Bishop enunciated; if we will reflect on it, we may at once turn his warning to practical account.

But we have a ready excuse for making that use of the Cholera, and similar visitations, which you would deem the heathen or Antichristian use. We say that the weal of the body must always be subordinate to the weal of the soul; that if any calamity affords us an opportunity of awakening in men a desire for the salvation of the soul, we are guilty of a great sin when we neglect that opportunity. "Who has a right to set the mortal part above the immortal, to care for that which is doomed to perish in a few years, when that is at stake which is to last for ever and ever?"

The truth which is latent in this language ought not to be forgotten, whatever confusion may be in it. But since theological indistinctness, and an indifference to the great articles of faith, are the crimes which the Bishop of Oxford specially imputes to our time, I cannot overlook the remarkable instance of both which these popular pleas for the soul supply. Is the body, then, to perish in a few years? Is it not to live for ever? What, then, becomes of the words, "I believe in the Resurrection of the Body?" What becomes of that fifteenth chapter of the Corinthians with which we console the mourners beside every grave? People would be utterly shocked if they were supposed to deny this doctrine; and yet they do deny it habitually. They make a religion of

denying it.   They represent three-score years and
ten as the limit of life in the body ; they contrast
it with something else which is to last on for ever.

This cannot be the way of stating the difference between that which we design to exalt and
that we design to depress, if the Gospel is true ;
this must be a heathen conception of the difference.   But, heathen or not, we all feel that there
is a vast difference between the senses and the
physical energies which we have in common with
other animals and that which belongs to us as
men.   Both may be destined to life.   The argument
of Butler for continuance applies equally to each
were there no higher testimony on the subject.
But clearly the life in one and the other cannot be
the same ; there must be a profound sense in the
language—whether adopted by modern preachers
or ancient philosophers—which sets the soul's life
above the animal life.   The phraseology may not
be scriptural, may even be curiously the reverse
of scriptural.   But that it should have been
accepted so generally by divines who are most conversant with Scripture, and who have intended to
do the Scriptures honour, is a reason why we
should not cast it aside until we have extracted
the full virtue out of it, nor then unless we can
exchange it for some better language.

Doddridge and other excellent men have traced a process which they describe as the rise and progress of religion in the soul. The man is startled out of a dream of unconsciousness. He begins to ask who he is, whence he came, whither he is going. No doubt you may say that such a man is occupied about his soul. He will easily adopt your phraseology. He is occupied about something which may have that name or any other you like to give it. He knows that that which puzzles and torments him is *himself*. He is an awful being; he is not like the birds and beasts about him. What, then, is he? Must not the answer be given by some one above him —some one who knows him? He is sure that it must. He has heard often that his Maker has spoken to men, has revealed Himself to them, has told them they were wandering from Him, has bidden them arise and come to him. He now accepts the tidings as true. They answer to that which has been stirring in him. He has been sought, and he has been found. He confesses that it is even so. He begins, in the strictest sense, to *believe* in One who is about his bed and his board, and is spying out his ways. The power at which he trembled becomes the object of his confidence. His life is altogether a different life from that of the body—that of the animal. For a time he is disposed to scorn that; it looks so mean in comparison. By degrees he feels that the higher life ought to make, that it does make, the lower far more intelligible, far more beautiful, far more sacred. But they must never be confused. He may not be able to discover the right way of distinguishing them. The New Testament tells him the way. It tells him that there is a life of God, an eternal life, which was with the Father, and which Christ has manifested to us. To possess this, cannot be the privilege of the animal nature. It must be for the *man* who was made in God's image.

Am I, being a man, really created for this knowledge, for this enjoyment? And may I not *lose* this knowledge, this enjoyment? Am I not every moment in danger of losing it? Are not my fellow-creatures in the like danger? Have not I been—are not most men—even ignorant that there is such a life as this, quite indifferent about possessing it? Behind the vision of this eternal life, there rises the vision of an eternal death. It is the dark terrible background to all that looks so glorious, so satisfying to the yearnings of a human being. Apprehensions of it, likenesses of it, have evidently haunted all ages, all countries. But the full sense of it, the complete terror of it, is reserved for those on whom the fullest light has dawned. Till the man knows a little of his own capacity for good, he has no dream of his capacity for evil. Then there ascends out of the deepest caverns of his spirit the cry to be delivered out of the bitter pains of eternal death.

But to WHOM does the cry ascend? Is it to the Author of the eternal death? Will *he* raise any creature out of it? Or is it to the Author, the Revealer of the eternal life? to Him who has manifested that life in His only begotten Son, that men might know it, and have the bliss of it? This, my friend, is the question of English divinity at the present day. The vagueness, the theological indistinctness which is over us, gathers about this point. It is not the question whether there is an eternal death. It is whether God the Creator has devised and prepared that eternal death for his creatures. Or whether we may say of this, as of the other death, He is the Redeemer from it; He is the Author of life— only of life.

Here, again, we may appeal to you—we may ask you to teach us again some of the earliest lessons of our childhood. The godfather and

godmother, at baptism, in the name of the child,
renounce the Devil and all his works. They
verily declare that the Devil is not the lord and
master of that infant; that he has no claim or
right whatsoever over it; that it has been redeemed by its true Father, for His service. The
words have become to us as an idle tale. Some
of us tremble to speak them; some do not
tremble, because they seem such an unmeaning
formula. You know what it is for men to
acknowledge an evil spirit as their lord and
master, and the lord and master of their children.
You know what it is for men to tremble before
such a power, which is plotting their destruction here and hereafter; which they must try
to conciliate, if they can, by offerings and
sacrifices, or by the intercession of milder
deities, who may have a favour to some of them.
Unless you can tell those to whom you speak,
that there is a Father, who has created them
and all mankind; that there is a Son, who has
redeemed them and all mankind; that there is a
Spirit of goodness and truth, who is stronger
than the Spirit of evil and falsehood; you must
hold your tongue; you cannot preach the Gospel
which you have been sent to preach. But if you
can do this, there can be no parleying for you

with the question whether God means the death of any man; whether He is the author of death to the body or the spirit of any whom He has formed. You must proclaim Him simply, broadly, absolutely, as the God of salvation—as the God who has sent His Son into the world for the very purpose of saving us out of all death, of bringing us to the highest life of which He has made us capable. Trust, entire trust, in Him, is the right state for body and spirit. But the spirit exercises the trust; the body only receives the blessing of it in the freedom of all its powers and energies.

These lessons, I say, we want at home; you must help us in recovering them. If we do, we shall regain all that was vital and fervent in the teachings of those who have dwelt most on the salvation of the soul; we shall escape their morbid habit of poring over the conditions of the soul; the coldness which follows the excitement of hope and fear respecting it; the hypocrisy, the infidelity which is the consequence of that reaction. The words of the Psalmist, " *Say to my soul I am thy salvation,*" will come forth with ever new force to the man who is struggling to rise out of his own dreariness and despondency. And yet he will understand St. Paul's contempt for the mere *soulish* man, his sympathy with the spiritual man.

3

Each of us is prone to be soulish; to be shut up
in himself. Is not that what the Devil would have
us be? To be entirely shut up in self, is not this
the deepest damnation? To be spiritual men, to
seek that which is above us, to drink in the life
which is for all—is not this the blessing to which
God invites us, is not this His salvation?

The habit of self-contemplation which our
language about the soul is so apt to foster, is
one of which you would warn us, knowing to
what superstitions, to what dark and cruel contrivances of mortification, of so-called purification,
it has led Yogis and Dervishes. But if by the
Soul is meant the organ of thought, you would say
to us as earnestly, "This must be awakened: we
must call upon God to awaken it, for we cannot.
To make men *think*—oh! how hard this is!" Yes!
my friend, you pray to the living God that He will
enable heathens to think, that He will break the
bonds which hinder them from thinking. Only
when they begin to think freely, can they renounce
the Devil's service and enter upon His. And what
a lesson is that for us! We have learnt to connect free-thinking with Atheism! We warn our
sons against free-thinking! I am well persuaded
that we must one and all, laymen and priests,
repent of this language, and of the temper which

it expresses.   Unless we have much more free-thinking in our land than we have now or ever had, I fear we shall sink into Devil-worshippers : unless the clergy cultivate free-thought, instead of checking it, they will become the Devil's ministers, and not God's.—Ever yours, &c.

LETTER IV.

FREE-THINKING.

My dear Friend,—What I said about free-think-ing at the end of my last letter will scandalize many persons whom I should grieve to scandalize. But I dare not suppress it; for their sakes I dare not. For the sake of all the truths, which I am pledged by my vows as an English clergyman to contend for, I dare not. That the freest thought should be supposed to be atheistical thought; that it should be the habit of our time to identify one with the other; that the most religious people should adopt the opinion, and take every opportunity of endorsing it: this appears to me the most frightful example of theological indistinctness which can be imagined. It must *terminate* in that confusion which the Bishop of Oxford predicts as the result of theological indistinctness. Does it not *begin* in that confusion? Is not a secret suspicion that God is the Evil Spirit, at the root of the notion that if men were freer to think they would set Him at defiance ?

" But is not the natural heart at enmity with God ? Does not the Bible say so ? " Undoubtedly it does. And the same Bible not only says, but testifies by its whole history, that the natural heart is prone to slavery ; that men, if they follow their own inclinations, sink of course into slaves. Because there is this tendency in men, and they know and feel that there is, they have recognized any who have won freedom for them—and who in winning it had to struggle with all kinds of opposition from those whom they benefited—as sent by some gods, as having the surest divine credentials. The Bible says that *the* God, the God of gods, the King of kings, is the author of freedom ; that men murmur and rebel against Him because they prefer bondage ; that all the acts of His providence and government are to overcome that preference, to give them an appetite and zeal for the freedom wherewith He makes them free.

That external freedom is the result of internal freedom ; that the first is sure to perish, where the second has been lost ; that a man may be free when he is in chains because his thoughts are

free : these are sayings which we have all repeated. We have supposed that in repeating them
we were showing our reverence for the benefactors
of the earth, for the martyrs of God. We have
associated this freedom with faith ; we have said
that men could defy visible terrors because they
could find their refuge in an unseen Helper. But
now it seems a point of religion that we should cast
this language aside, that we should adopt a habit
of mind which makes it worse than unmeaning.
The maxims which we are to learn are these :—
" Be afraid of thinking. Close your minds under
bolts and bars. Else this result is inevitable :
you will cease to believe." The feeling that
freedom of thought and unbelief are inseparable,
that one must generate the other is becoming
more and more fixed in those who are at war on
all other points. A man who denies Christianity
may be told by his religious friends that he is in
great peril, that he is trifling with his immortal
soul ; but they at once concede to him that he
has claimed a freedom to think which they dare
not exercise. They implore him to put on the
fetters which they wear. Such fetters, he is told,
are only painful at first—custom makes them
easy.

O damnable doctrine, preached in our pulpits,

preached in our market-places, leading indeed
to the perdition of men's souls, producing all
the worldliness of thought and practice which
religious men profess to hate and abjure, blight-
ing all that is strong, hopeful, faithful, in young
men, establishing some of them in the conviction
that all thought of unseen things must be unreal,
settling others in an impenetrable hypocrisy! Yes!
we have here the doctrine of Devils, which has
darkened the doctrine of the Son of God in all
parts and in all ages of Christendom, which has
substituted a heartless acquiescence for a living
faith, which every reformer who has sought to restore faith has found, and will ever find, the huge
dead-weight that is opposing him.   Thanks be
to the Almighty God, the God and Father of our
Lord Jesus Christ, for every instrument which
He has called forth to deliver the church and
mankind from this intolerable load.   We talk of
the French infidelity of the last century as if we
supposed that Voltaire and Diderot were men
who conquered God.   Such blasphemy may be
reasonable enough in those who do not believe
that God is, who suppose that He is a fiction
of priests.   We who hold that He is, that He
lives, that He has reigned, and does reign, and
will reign for ever, must confess that these men

were, consciously or unconsciously, willingly or
unwillingly, doing His work. They existed to
prove that He is not a fiction of the priests, since
whatever is that trembles and shrinks away, and
confesses by shrinking its own mortality; since
the canon of the inspired writer will always make
itself good—"Things which can be shaken are
taken away, that those which cannot be shaken
may remain." If we do not fully accept that
assertion, if we do not apply it to every part of
history, we evade the testimony of Scripture, we
do not confess the kingdom of God. If we do
accept it, we must hold that all emancipation of
thought, just so far as it has gone, has been
good; that its only fault has been that it has
not gone far enough. Our complaint should be
that the sceptic has not dared boldly enough to
face the problems of his own life, and of the
world's life, and to demand a solution of them;
that he has been too soon contented with the
lazy, cowardly conclusion that they are insoluble;
that he therefore lounges and falls asleep in his
carriage, and takes all things as they come, when
no such condition as this can be right for a creature which looks before and after; that he compli-
ments himself too soon on his freedom, whilst he
is still wearing shackles which the custom of the

time, or the tradition of the past, or the conceit
of his own mind, has fastened on him. Every
step he has taken out of mere acquiescence is a
step for which he and we should be thankful.
Every doubt which has been stirred within him is
a sign that there is something better for him than
to eat and drink and die. But any self-congratu-
lation upon this step, any boasting of the doubts
which make him restless, is unseemly, unrea-
sonable, ridiculous. It is excusable as against
us, since we have led him to count anything better than the repose to which we have
tempted him. It is not excusable as against
himself: it is inconsistent with his professions,
unworthy of his manhood.

What then ought we to do? Here, too, you
must be our teacher. Whatever form of heathenism you have to deal with, the most rude or the
most complicated, this problem will surely encounter you. That you should awaken suspicions about
old traditions, about existing customs and modes
of worship, is the necessity of your position.
You can fulfil no one task for which you were
sent out if you do not stir some thought, if you do
not kindle life where death has been. How this
should be done, is the question which you have
to ask yourself continually. That you *may* be the

means of producing a mere habit of scepticism—
a mere distrust of what is not true, without any
belief in that which is—you must be quite aware.
You faced that peril when you took your office
upon you. You were not ignorant that the mere
contact with Western civilization, with a people
trained in the notions and habits of modern
science, involved a great disturbance in the minds
of men brought up in the notions which the
natives of any idolatrous country count sacred.
You hoped that you might render the movement
which this collision makes inevitable less tremendous, that you might give the soul that had
become empty, swept, and garnished, something
to fill the niches from which the old images had
departed. You hoped this. Has it proved a vain
hope? Sometimes you will think so; sometimes
you will fancy that you have only aggravated
the mischief which you might have alleviated,
which you might even have cured. But you will
be least tormented by this suspicion, or you will
find the only refuge from it, when you say, " My
judgment is with my God. It is He who is
making these men impatient of their fetters. If
the fetters are not broken He will not be in any
of their thoughts; the dark spirit who strives
against Him will be in all of them. I will tell

them that freedom of thought comes from His inspiration ; that He will not leave them to the slumber, ruffled by fantastic dreams, which they choose ; that He calls them to light and liberty ; that if they feel any craving for these, they may know Who has put it within them, and Who can satisfy it."

Such lessons from you could not strike the supporters of missionary enterprises in Europe as strange. The enterprises must be abandoned if these lessons are not lawful, or if they are to be kept back from any idolater or any Mussulman. And are we not to learn them ? Are they not for the people of England and the clergy of England ? Merciful God ! art Thou then gone away wholly into the lands of the people who do not know Thee ? Are we, the people of Thy pasture, because we have Bibles and creeds and preachers, left without Thy presence ? When our young men become perplexed with questionings about the wonders of Thy universe and the mysteries of their own being, are we, the ministers of Thy Word, to tell them Thou art crushing and silencing their perplexities and desires for light ? Are we to bid them, in Thy name, choose death rather than life ? Are we not to tell them that Thy Word is with them, and

that He will teach them Thy fear and Thy worship, so that they shall not learn what Thou art
by our precept, but by thine own revelation?
Wilt Thou not cause the teachers of Thy people
to believe, as Apostles, Prophets, and Reformers
believed, that it is Satan who enslaves, and Thou
who makest free? I know, my friend, you will
join with me in the prayer for England and her
colonies, and for all whom she can guide by her
word or her example, that they may learn thus
to understand the purposes of their enemy and
of their Friend.—Ever yours, &c.

LETTER V.

FREEDOM OF CONSCIENCE.

MY DEAR FRIEND,—I said in my last letter that we should encourage men to desire much more freedom of thought than they ever desired ; that we should rebuke them only for being content with so little. The name of free-thinker, therefore, is one which we should honour in any one who claims it for himself : we should dispute his right to monopolize it. There is another claim which we listen to with more seeming respect, often with much concealed impatience and suspicion. When any one says that he is entitled to perfect freedom of conscience, we are apt to answer, " Oh, yes ! and you have it, as much as you can possibly require. Are you exposed to any penalties for your profession of belief, even of unbelief ? Do not our laws protect all alike ? Are not the greater part of the offices and privileges of the State open to all ? Liberty of conscience, indeed !

A very good phrase at elections; but when it is used in private conversation, it is commonly meant to disguise an incredulity which the speaker does not care to profess."

Now here is theological indistinctness in a very aggravated form. In the first place, if we attach any meaning to the word Conscience, if it stands for anything in our minds, how can the removal of outward restraints from it constitute its freedom? That there should not be such restraints is, doubtless, an unspeakable good; that the power of inducing my neighbour to lie, by motives of fear or hope, should be taken from me, is good for him, and still better for me. But his conscience may be still imprisoned, though I cannot imprison his body. If there is a conscience at all in him, its prison-house *must* be of a different kind from that which confines his limbs. He may be able to use those without the least check, and yet may be writhing in fetters. Surely men who read their Bibles, who read even ordinary religious books, should know this. And yet it is they who continually obliterate this distinction, who actually teach men that they ought to be well satisfied if the hangman and the policeman let them alone.

But, secondly: How *can* the claim for liberty of conscience be a claim for the privilege of being indifferent? It is the strongest assertion of a dreadful duty *not* to be indifferent. Acquiescence in a popular opinion is the obvious, easy, course for every man. The indifferent man at once drops into it—·why should he do otherwise? The man who speaks of his conscience alleges that he dares not acquiesce, that indifference is for him a dangerous, an impossible state. He appeals from the decisions of his fellow-creatures to a higher judgment throne, by whatever name he may describe that throne, whoever he may suppose to be seated upon it.

" Well, but if he should say that there is no one seated upon it, that he is his own judge?" A very dreadful opinion—alas! a very possible one. Men may say this; men do say it. Who have taught them to say it? who have led them to suppose that Christians adopt the saying as a true one? My friend, the confession must be made: we have done this. We have not recognized the cry for liberty of conscience as a genuine divine cry; as a cry to Him who has inspired it; as the cry of a spirit which feels that it cannot be tied and bound by rules which we have imposed upon it; that it has an unseen Ruler, whom it must feel after till it finds Him. That cry of the strong swimmer in his agony we have

mocked; we have treated it as presumptuous; we
have bade the sufferer think that he is left to himself, that there is no one at hand to help him.
He has taken us at our word. He has said,
" Then I am alone. The waves are too mighty
for me. I will strive as long as I can. It is your
teaching that I must sink at last."

Oh! we know not what we have been doing
whilst we have thus trifled with a precious form
of speech which is sealed with the blood of the
noblest patriots the world or the church has ever
had; whilst we have been complimenting ourselves on the wit and cleverness with which we
have exhibited it as a mere political platitude or
a trick of unbelief. We know not what we have
been doing. For we *must* in pulpits talk about the
conscience; we must try to stir the consciences
of our hearers; we must speak of the deliverance
of the conscience from a heavy burden. Those
pulpit words and those week-day words seem as
if they had some relation to each other. We are
careful to tell others and to tell ourselves that
they have none. The conscience which the man
speaks of, and for which he claims freedom, is
not the conscience we have to do with. What is
it, then? Are we only talking technical divinity?
Are we not speaking to human beings in their

own dialect? Is all our preaching a mere scheme for calling forth a something which is not? Are we to lay bare the tricks and deceptions of the heart—to bring it face to face with the Searcher of the heart—or to cheat it with an ambiguous phraseology, which must make all the webs that it weaves for itself a thousandfold more intricate and hopeless?

The reaction on ourselves is fearful. We, too, divide our Sunday from our week-day conscience; the last is often the simpler and honester of the two. Yet we complain, and with reason, that the week-day conscience of the religious shopkeeper or politician is not what we should have expected from his Sunday professions. We make abortive attempts to restore the connexion. Must it not first be fully restored in us! Must we not listen to the warnings of the Bishop and ask whether we have not been confounding the true Lord with the Spirit of lies; whether our duplicity about the conscience has not its root in this duplicity? Has not each of *us* heard One saying to him, " *Behold I stand at the door and knock.*" Is He not a friend who seeks to set us free from the impostures to which we have yielded? Has not each of us heard another voice, one which bids him despair of such

4

an emancipation, which tells him that the only
safety is in fresh and more cunning impostures
to support those which have proved ineffectual?
Here is the very mystery of Conscience—that
which justifies all that has ever been said of its
grandeur, all that has ever been said of its defile-
ment. If we know something of that mystery of
the conscience, if we are conscious of the presence
of One whose still small voice can make us tremble
more than all thunders and earthquakes—conscious of the presence of one who would stop our
ears to that voice, who would drown it in the
world's noises, we can speak, it should be always
with fear and trembling, to our fellow-men of
that which is passing in them. We can now and
then arouse them by our words to perceive the
facts of their life, which theories about the conscience try feebly to represent. We can always
assure them that the power is not in our words,
but in that Word who is nigh to the heart at all
times when no mortal lips can speak to the ear.
But if we do this we are bound to respect all
recognitions of this truth which come forth in
any form, even in the forms which are most
affronting to us, even in the form of apparent
defiance to our statements. The assertion of any
man that he cannot follow our teaching because

there is a conscience within him which demands
a higher and more satisfactory teaching should be
reverenced by us. We know that he does want
better and more satisfactory teaching than ours.
As the ministers of God, we should earnestly tell
him that he has it. Any cry for freedom of
conscience, though it means freedom from our
opinions and judgments, must be sacred in our
ears. The man who utters this cry may discover
hereafter that he has need of a more complete
emancipation—an emancipation from his own
judgments and opinions as well as ours. But
let us honour what has been given him. God is
teaching him secretly and by degrees that there
is a Spirit which would guide him from opinions
into truth. Let us not mar the effect of that
Divine education by our hasty and blundering
discouragement. Let us confess with our hearts
what we say with our lips in church, and let us, if
we can, confess it to each man with our lips,
that we believe in this Spirit of truth, that He
is a guide for us and for him. Let us tell
him that the Spirit of truth is also the Spirit
of liberty, the Deliverer of the conscience from
its bondage. And when we speak of the seeds
of slavery which are continually springing up
in his heart and in ours, let us affirm fear-

lessly and constantly, " The enemy hath done this."

My friend, though it may seem strange that you who dwell amidst so much darkness should be able to instruct us who boast of so much light, yet I do believe that, about this twilight of the conscience, no experience will be more profitable than yours. As to that question of outward restraints, of State penalties, it is impossible that you can fall into the mistake of identifying the absence of these with freedom of the conscience. You know in what bondage the consciences of heathens may be when they have been brought under the protection of a Government which has no motive to enforce by penalties any of the religious influences that are acting upon them, and yet, which is extremely cautious of interfering with those influences. You welcome the security which a civilized Power gives you by not *obliging* heathens to practise immoral superstitions, by prohibiting direct crimes against the peace of society. You believe that this security would be diminished, not increased, if the Government encouraged the natives to desert their old superstitions, precisely because you think such a course would tend to corrupt not to liberate their consciences. These are great steps in that wisdom which should belong to the politician when he is brought into contact with the opinions of any class of men. Your theological lore, if you use it rightly, will as little interfere with the political lore, as with the medical. It may help the first as much as the second.

But then as to the deeper question—as to the way of freeing the conscience from those chains which the statesman cannot loosen, which he may often through overdoing help to rivet. Cannot you give us some counsel about this? You must perceive that neither the weight of a long tradition, nor the laziness of habit, could avail to sustain the numberless practices and notions which most enfeeble and debase the minds of those to whom you preach, if there was not in them a conscience of evil, the perpetual tormenting sense of something wrong, something that may expose them to the vengeance of a power which takes account of the wrong and will punish it. To this conscience of sin every priest and soothsayer practically addresses himself: if it were not there, he would prescribe as much in vain as the physician would prescribe remedies if there were no pain or sickness. All the multiplied devices for getting rid of the consequences which may follow the evil, as well as of the sense of

present pain which accompanies it—if possible of
the remembrances of the past which haunt the
ill-doer—all these of course assume that the evil
itself cannot be uprooted, that that is incurable.
And yet the very man who submits to this dismal
conclusion, and tortures himself perpetually while
he submits, has a conscience of a Good, of a Right,
which is close to him, which he might lay hold of,
which would raise him out of the evil whereby he
is tied and bound.   What have you gone out for
but to speak to this conscience of Good, to bear
witness that it has not told a false tale ; that the
Good of which it whispers has met with it, has
come down to it, is on its right hand, that it might
be delivered, not from the consequences of the
evil, not from the pain of the evil, but from the
evil itself: from that evil which is both past and
present, and future, which has in it a permanent
and eternal nature, which can only be shaken off
by trust in the Eternal Good ?

   Yes, this is your Gospel, the Gospel of Him
who took our nature, that He might redeem us
from all iniquity: the Gospel of Him in whom all
are commanded to trust, that they may be found
in Him not having their own righteousness, but
that which is of God *upon* faith.*   If you can only

---

* Phil. c. iii. v. 9 : ἐπὶ τῇ πίστει.

recognize a conscience of evil in any heathen or any Mussulman, all you can do is to provide him with new contrivances for escaping the punishment of his evil. And all those contrivances, derived from one scheme of Divinity or another, will make his conscience more slavish, more unclean. If you can recognize a conscience of good in him—if you have courage to address that, you will bring forth in him the sense of evil, the hatred of evil, as he never had it before: he will see that it is a foul thing, natural indeed to him, but never meant for him. He was created after God in righteousness and true holiness; the Son of Man is the Lord of him and of every man: owning Him as his Lord, he has the righteousness which makes him a true man.

Here surely is the secret which St. Paul was taught, of keeping a conscience void of offence before God and man. Here is that freedom of conscience to which all feel that they have a right, and which we have discouraged them from demanding. The Bishop of Oxford has told us why we have discouraged them. We are losing the distinction between God the source of good and the Spirit who would drag us into all evil.— Yours, &c.

LETTER VI.

FREEDOM OF THE WILL.

MY DEAR FRIEND,—Free-thinking we are wont utterly to denounce; freedom of conscience is at least a suspicious phrase; but the freedom of the Will it is respectable, even orthodox, to defend. Arminians charge Calvinists with impugning it: Calvinists are, in general, anxious to repel the imputation. They do not, they say, reject free-will in any sense which implies that a man is not responsible for his actions, and will not be punished if his actions are bad.

The history of the debate on this subject is curious. The most vehement assertors of free-will in the century when opinions about it most affected practical life in Great Britain, were the defenders of the Royal prerogative; the champions of political liberty denounced Arminians as its foes. They perceived in their doctrine precisely that demand for subjection to mere visible authority against which they protested in the Papist. If we consider that paradox, we obtain much light upon the circumstances of that period; I believe, also, upon the relation of theology to politics in all periods.

Practically, the defenders of the hierarchy in the sixteenth century were maintaining this thesis —that God had transferred His government to certain ecclesiastical rulers, and that He only interfered from time to time by miracles to prove that they had the power which they claimed for themselves, and to punish those who resisted them. The Reformers affirmed that God was the Lord still, as He had ever been; that He was ruling on His own earth; that He was then breaking asunder the bonds by which His people were bound, as much as He had broken the bonds of the Israelites when they were making bricks for Pharaoh's treasure-houses. This belief lay at the root of the Reformation—I might say it *was* the Reformation. It was seen that the Old Testament did not speak only or chiefly of material fetters: the slavery of the Israelites was in their hearts and wills; they longed for the Egyptian flesh-pots; they chose captivity. None could have rescued them from the outward tyrant but He who was the Master both

of Pharaoh and of them; none but He could
have overcome that more terrible inward slavery.
The Reformers read this in the sacred history;
they felt it in themselves. A hundred princes,
German or English, might have risen against the
Pope; but if his material power were broken—
if he was shut up in the Castle of St. Angelo,
not for a few days, but perpetually—would their
spirits be the freer from the yoke which he had
put upon them? No! men's wills, left to themselves, must always have some oppressor or other.
The unseen oppressor will always have some new
instrument ready to do his work; if there were
none, he would be himself their master. If any
became free indeed—if any could serve the true
God in truth, *He* must have emancipated wills
which were naturally enslaved.

These are the maxims of Luther's famous
work against Erasmus. They are imbedded, no
doubt, in many angry and violent phrases, such
as may be expected in all controversy, and which
do not become better when they are rendered
into the less honest, not less cruel, dialect of our
century. And these same maxims, passing from
metaphysical theology into politics, made the Calvinist, even more than the Lutheran, so powerful
an ally of civil liberty in Scotland, Holland, Eng-

land; if it may not be rather said—as Hume has
said—that he gave civil liberty its impulse and
direction. For *this* Calvinism involved no miserable
waiting for some angel to go down and trouble the
waters. The waters were troubled. God, not an
angel, had troubled them. He had come down to
fight with His enemies. He invited men to fight
with Him. Woe to those who joined the opposing
host; though according to the judgment of mortal
eyes, it was ten thousand times stronger!

And then came the doctors with their explanation of this mystery of the Divine and human
will, and the action of one upon the other. An
explanation how ingenious, how logical, how
miserable!—one which must take the form of
an apology for God: an attempt to show why
certain wills were enfranchised, and certain wills
were left in bondage. Out of this attempt springs
the dogmatic or school Calvinism. By it the
Divine will is resolved into mere sovereignty;
the human will becomes no will at all. The old
Calvinists, who knew that this could not be the explanation—that it was not an explanation to their
own hearts, or to their nation—strove hard against
this logical necessity. Knox is furious against
the opponents who dared to libel him and his
friends by saying that they made sovereignty, and

not righteousness, the ground of the Divine predestination.

The protest was sincere; it came forth in act.
Knox defied sovereignty for the sake of righteousness. A Mary Stuart, or a Charles IX., or a
Philip II., clothed with infinite power, would
not have approached nearer to his idea of God—
would have represented exactly his idea of a
supreme Devil. And men who bowed before
such a being because they thought he must con-
quer, would have exactly fulfilled his idea of the
apostate world, the apostate Christendom, from
which he exhorted God's elect people in Scotland to come forth and be separate. He asserted,
therefore, a will in God, which was the very
reverse of a mere sovereign will; he appealed to
a will in man which was the very *reverse* of a
mere nature only capable of being moved by
some violent force. The Arminian school, nevertheless, could prove satisfactorily that the Calvinists
had in their arguments, often in their very words,
reduced each will to this negative condition. In
Holland the Calvinists answered the demonstra-
tion by imprisonments, confiscations, deaths: so
confirming the charge which they intended to
silence; proving that it did faithfully express their
purpose when they had power in their hands;

that they did *then* proclaim God as a Tyrant Ruler, and the will of man as something which it was His pleasure only to annihilate or to torment. But Arminianism in England came to be in the ascendant; the king, who had cherished Calvinism as a dogma and as an assertion of the highest form of prerogative, found that, neither here nor in Scotland, was the confession of supreme authority in a living God favourable to the notion that that authority was transferred to him. He learnt from Laud that the champion of free-will was his most practical protector against the insolent notion that subjects might appeal from his tribunal to a higher one, or expect any reversal of the sentence which had gone forth from the inferior. *Such* a free-will the patriots in the House of Commons denounced as their worst foe; unless there was a Will in the Heavens which could set right human doings, which might be invoked when human government was utterly perverse and monstrous, they felt that they and that England must despair.

But they triumphed. Calvinism had here also the trial of success, and again all its darker features began to show themselves. Then came the great champion of Necessity, who provoked and confounded Calvinists and Arminians equally.

Hobbes hated the first with a thorough hatred, because they had overthrown State decrees and its order in the name of a Divine will. He scorned the second for their inconclusive efforts to maintain a certain mysterious responsibility in men to a Power which, as they confessed by their acts and in their political theories, had delegated its functions to earthly magistrates. The Puritan and the High Churchman were equally tormented by the philosopher of Malmesbury; each saw some of his own feathers in the fatal dart which was striking him. In the next age, Butler perceived, with a keen and wise instinct, how only Hobbes could be encountered. He must be left in possession of his logical victory. On the ground of practice, in the actual battle of life, men confess themselves to be responsible voluntary creatures: a necessity is laid upon the Necessitarian to join in that acknowledgment. The disciple of Hobbes had no doubt maintained the adverse position upon a similar ground. The champion of free-will, he said, in the act of vindicating it, confesses a motive, and so a necessity, by which he is bound. There is something comical in this interchange of phrases and arguments. Each disputant must have a sense of humour when he mounts his opponent's theory, and, as in village donkey races, wins by being hindmost. But the comedy is confined to the *statement* of the fact; deep tragedy lies in the fact itself. When the disputant on either side is driven from books to life, he must become serious. The disciple of Butler could rest in no dogmatic security. He had committed himself to the trial of battle. He might be compelled in the midst of the fight to change rapiers with his opponent. In Butler's day many a man had this experience. The Methodist preaching was in one sense a passionate proclamation of free-will. All were asked to come to the waters and drink, to believe and be saved. In another sense it was a passionate proclamation that only God could convert the will, that till He converted it the will must be tied and bound. Nothing was more natural or reasonable than that the Methodist leaders should divide on this issue; that a vehement, not a dry scholastic, Arminianism should grow up under the hands of Wesley, an equally vehement, an equally un-scholastic, Calvinism under the hands of Whit-field. Each was the complement of the other. The dogmatists of each school might be furious against its opponents, might deem them worthy of being consigned to outer darkness. Yet neither could have existed without the other ; and the dogmatism of each, except as it had the very grave effect of producing bitterness and ill-will, was of the slightest possible significance. The American Edwards stood on a different ground. His arguments occupy an important place in the theological and political history of his country. But in England the speculation may be almost overlooked : the practical controversy was of the greatest interest. The *action* of Free-will and of Predestination might be seen in crowds of the poorest and the richest people ; the interpretation of that action which proceeded from the partisans of one or the other, was confessed to be inadequate by those who clung to it most eagerly.

And, therefore, what remains to us when the excitement of the battle is over ? I am afraid the Bishop of Oxford has told us the truth in this case also. There is no longer on either side the dread of a mighty Enemy who is seeking to enslave the will, no longer the cry to a mightier Friend to deliver the will. As long as this dread lasted, as this cry was raised, no amount of perplexity or confusion about terms could involve a hopeless moral confusion. The moment of pacification is the dangerous moment. Then there is much pleasant embracing. The Arminian

agrees to admit just so much of necessity as may
limit the power of the divine will to save fallen
spirits. The Calvinist admits just so much of
free-will as may account for the refusal of the
majority of men to embrace the Gospel. So we
have sermons—probably some of the cleverest
delivered in English pulpits—which are occupied
with proving how men disable themselves from
believing the divine message by the indulgence of
evil habits: sermons full of undoubted truth, yet
which, thus barely stated, must drive us all to
despair. For to which of us does it not apply?
Which of us is not in continual peril of harden-
ing his heart against belief, of strengthening his
will against the discovery of its perversion? What
men are more prone to do this than we who are
conversant with all the phrases and dogmas of
religion, who are continually speaking of them to
our fellows? It is all true; but is there no voice
to tell us how that natural downward progress
may be arrested, no one to speak of a Power
mightier than that, which is drawing us upward?
Oh, yes, there are such: men who proclaim that
the grace of God is sufficient for all things, able
to blot out all transgressions, to create a clean
heart and a right spirit in the most evil. Beautiful tidings! how one longs to accept them in

5

their length and breadth. No! that may not be.
The *believer* knows that this is so; he has this
blessed experience of the power of God's grace.
The poor unbeliever is utterly cast off from it.
Sermons of this kind, sometimes, no doubt, mere
repetitions of phrases that have been learnt by
rote from books or living teachers, but sometimes full of the genuine experience of the
speaker's own heart, testifying of what he has
known—are heard in English churches. They
might be a help to numbers in all states of mental
darkness, of moral debasement, were it not for
this frightful limitation, this huge practical contradiction. The grace of God is made not the
ground of man's belief, but dependent upon it.
Trust in God's righteousness was that which
raised men at the Reformation out of trust in
their own doings. They owned that they were
good for nothing, and they must therefore cling
to Him who was good for everything. Now the
belief that they are good for nothing, that He
is good for everything, is to be an excuse for
self-glorification, a reason for saying, "We are
not as other men are!" O strange subtlety of
the Evil Spirit,—what Arminian or Calvinistical
dogmas are a protection against him? What but
an entire belief in that Will which has overcome

him and made a mockery of him? Does not every true Arminian, every true Calvinist, confess, "To that Will I must betake myself, because it is almighty to save; because my will, whether I call myself believer or unbeliever, Christian or heathen, must become the victim of the evil will, unless there is a Will that all should be saved, that all should come to the knowledge of the truth."

How far the denial of this truth has gone—the truth I mean either of God's Will, or of His power to raise wills or spirits out of their bondage to sin and death—I think none of us know. I could quote passages from Episcopal sermons, from Episcopal charges, which to all appearance make the fall of Adam, or the depravity of man, an insurmountable obstacle to the triumph of the divine will; supposing, I mean, it is such a will to save as the Scripture affirms it to be. I have seen other sermons and charges in which it appeared to be treated as a bold assumption of man's reason to say of this will what the Bible does say of it in express words: a daring impiety to suppose that the prayer for such a will to prevail can be answered. But I have no wish to fix so bad a meaning upon the authors of these passages. I rejoice to believe that they would disclaim it: my only object, if I produced them, would be to show how far the theological indistinctness which the Bishop of Oxford laments has penetrated, how near we all are to the confusion which he so rightly deems the most horrible of all. And that object may be far better accomplished if each one of us is stirred up to observe this indistinctness in himself, to resolve in God's strength that he will not bear with it, to ask that the contrast between God and Satan may stand out before him with something of the clearness in which it will appear when the darkness is past, and we are brought into Christ's full daylight. I know in myself—I think you must know in yourself—how great the temptation is to make the resistance of other men's wills, still more the resistance of our own will, to that which we feel and confess to be the right will, an argument for the impotence of this, and for the transcendent power of that which defies it. Who can charge this unbelief upon another? Who is not often mastered by it, when he is flattering himself most that all is well with him, when he is fullest of indignation against his neighbour's incredulity? But it *is* unbelief, the essential, radical unbelief. If we succumb to it, all is over with us : our work is a lie, our existence is a lie.

If this habit of mind, which has so nearly got

possession of us, is not shaken off, your occupation, my dear friend, is gone. Let us state the question fairly to ourselves. You are dealing with wills, with spirits, not with stones or animals. These wills or spirits are not free. It is idle to pretend that they are. They are fast bound in misery and iron. Has their Creator so bound them? Does He wish them so to be bound? Can He break their bonds asunder? When you find the answers to these questions share them with us! We cannot live unless we know them. I have not written to you about the freedom of the will because I wished to renew a dreary, interminable discussion: I have written of it because the whole subject of CONVERSION, abroad and at home, all that is most practical in your business and ours, is involved in it. That subject will occupy us in the next letter.—Faithfully yours, &c.

LETTER VII.

CONVERSION.

MY DEAR FRIEND,—You have gone out to convert idolaters or Mahometans. Here in England we are taught that it is our duty to aim at the conversion of profligates, of infidels, of Jews. A majority of English churchmen say that it would be very desirable to convert Roman Catholics; not a few try to convert members of different Protestant sects, who, as they express it, have separated themselves from our fold. The most devout men and women amongst ourselves say that there is a large body of unconverted people, who are neither Jews nor Romanists, nor profligates, whose conduct is correct, who observe punctually all the outward services of religion, who are zealous against outward infidelity, who dislike Dissenters. They may be staunch churchmen, they may be clergymen, they may be high ecclesiastics. These men, it is said, are in danger of their souls like the others; it is our duty to labour for their conversion.

When we hear these different applications of the word, we are forced to ask ourselves, "Has it the same sense in all of them? Or is it an ambiguous, deceitful word, which takes its shape and colour from each new subject which it touches?" The first and last uses of the phrase are those which seem to stand out in the most glaring contrast to each other. The difference between them is urgently insisted on by moderate men. "You did not mean that the worthy squire and parson of our parish, if they are a little worldly, need conversion of the same kind as one who accepts the Vedas or the Koran? Such a notion is extravagant and mischievous." Generally, a person who had expressed a strong opinion that the squire and the parson in question are unconverted, gives way to the objection. "No, he did not mean to go that length. Conversion from any form of false religion to Christianity must, he thinks, be different in kind from the conversion of one who has been baptized and brought up as a Christian to a better life." Well, then, is the conversion of these respectable men the same thing with the conversion of a murderer? There will be more hesitation in the answer to this question; but probably it will ultimately be conceded that there is a difference in this case also. There may be a little awkward attempt to maintain that the difference is in degree and not in kind; after a little pressing that refinement will be abandoned as unpractical.

Neither of these concessions would have been made by a fervent Wesleyan of the last age; they would be resisted by many young preachers in the Church of England, as well as among the Dissenters, now. For they would not only feel that the word was in peril of losing all its force through a series of explanations and qualifications; they would also recollect that the case of conversion which is most prominent in the New Testament—the one to which we instinctively refer for an illustration of the divine significance of conversion—was not the case of a profligate, or of one who rejected the faith of his country; but of one who, as touching the righteousness of the law, was blameless, who was zealous without measure for the traditions of his fathers. Must Saul of Tarsus then be given up as that example of God's ways to all disobedient and rebellious men, which he told his son Timothy that he was?

There are some to whom such a question

would offer little difficulty. They would say,
" St. Paul's conversion was of course an excep-
tional event. It has been recognized as such by
all writers on the miracles of the apostolical age.
No one has reason to expect in these days that a
light should shine on him from Heaven, that he
should hear the voice of Jesus, that he should be
blind for three days, that an Ananias should be
sent to lay his hands on him and bid him arise
and be baptized. These are strange incidents,
the signs of an apostolical vocation, the prepa-
ration for a great and unusual work."

Be it so: all this is ordinarily taken for
granted, rightly taken for granted. The incident
did belong to a particular man and a particular
time. Men who have attached most importance
to the outward incidents of their own conversions, have not supposed that those of the Apostle
were repeated for them. Those who have studied
the Apostle's reports of his conversion, and his
Epistles, have been most disposed to dwell on the
internal change, the change of mind and purpose,
which caused the great wonder to him. But it is
so much the more remarkable—the strangeness
of his case being admitted, being even insisted
on by Christian writers — that we should all
have turned to this conversion as a typical

one, by which the origin, nature, and effects
of every conversion might be tested. There
was that first obvious characteristic of Saul's
history to which I have already alluded—that his
morals were exemplary, his religious sect the
straitest, his zeal the most fervent *for* that which
appeared to him his country's orthodoxy, *against*
a heresy which, as he thought, would break down
all barriers between the true faith and the
heathenism of the world. Such observations
furnished the evangelical preacher with a variety
of appeals to the consciences of those who were
going about to establish a righteousness of their
own, and were not seeking to be clothed with the
perfect righteousness of Christ. Yet in a tract
written by an accomplished Scotch layman of the
evangelical school, I read very recently an application of St. Paul's story to the case of a man
who had been suddenly aroused from a course of
depravity and dishonesty and had become a
zealous preacher. The *principle* of conversion
set forth in the journey to Damascus struck this
layman—who was certainly not a careless student
of Scripture—as illustrated by the change in a man
utterly unlike the Apostle in all his propensities
and outward conduct. Again, strange as it
might appear to connect so passionate a champion

of religion with unbelief, we have that cause assigned by the Apostle for his persecution of the Nazarenes—assigned not to aggravate, but to qualify the guilt of it: "I did it in ignorance and unbelief."

Every believer in Jesus, I suppose, whose mind is much occupied about the conversion of the Jews, individually or nationally, turns to the record of the conversion of this Hebrew of the Hebrews as the great warrant for his hopes. And every one who is engaged in your work will recollect the words in which St. Paul speaks of God being pleased to manifest His Son in him, that he might preach Him among the Gentiles. It may seem an anticlimax to pass from these cases to those special uses of the word Conversion which have prevailed among Romanists when they have spoken of secular men or women as converted to the monastic or religious life; or to the special use of it among Protestants when they speak of bringing Romanists to their faith; but it would be easy to show that the first draw their precedents scarcely more from later saints than from him who counted all things but loss that he might win Christ; and that the second habitually quote him as the grand and original example of deliverance from traditions and will-worship. So that we may affirm boldly that all the most apparently inconsistent applications of the word Conversion are, by the consent of the parties who make them, referred to this as to a test or standard. All—however they may differ from each other—confess that the idea of conversion universally can be best deduced from this particular instance.

Those who recognize, as I do, a divine instinct in this strange unanimity, will carefully consider what we are told of Saul's conversion by the person who knew most about it, and then will ask themselves whether his statement does not interpret and reconcile the partial views which have distracted us. I cannot say that the result will be in all respects satisfactory. I do not pretend that it may not lay bare some hollownesses in our hearts which we should be glad to hide; but the office of every preacher of repentance and conversion is to exalt vallies and level hills. If that effect should be produced on any of us, we shall have another test of the soundness of our method.

1. To say that St. Paul speaks of his conversion as the direct work of God may sound like a dreary commonplace. But it is a commonplace which may be worthy of serious reflection. For

have we not an undefined suspicion that this was one of the circumstances which make his case unlike any that occur in our age? Are we not inclined to express ourselves somewhat in this way:—"Oh, of course, ultimately all influences on men's minds are from God; but here was a case of direct divine interference." Why do we consider it so? Is it, then, the visible light, or the apparition, which we suppose converted Saul? Were not these the *signs* of the work which took place in him—the tokens to him that the unseen God was stopping him in his course? We do not surely attribute to them the work itself? We do not mean that the power which restrained him or changed him was in them? Our answer must be distinct—"Yes," or "No." Loose phrases, such as "Not quite that," "Not that altogether," are insincere and bewildering. If we say "Yes," I will tell you what we shall do, supposing we care for the condition of our fellow-men. We shall despair of obtaining *such* sights and sounds as we imagine were effectual on the mind of St. Paul, but we shall aim at producing some tolerable imitation of them.* We shall try to

---

* I need scarcely remind my readers of the excellent description of a revival meeting in Mrs. Stowe's *Dred.*

surround those whom we wish to convert with some startling scenery, with some influences that may alarm them. We shall depend somewhat on powerful rhetoric; much on a machinery which may affect the nerves, especially of women. All these will occur to us as a reasonable approximation to the kind of agency before which Saul bowed. But if we think clearly and distinctly within ourselves thus: " Saul bowed to the voice of the living God speaking to him—not to his eyes, but to *him.* Saul's will surrendered itself at last to the Will of his Creator—to the Will which had been sustaining him, and was sustaining every creature:" then you will begin to understand his account of his experience both before and after that crisis in his history; then you will see why he could testify so simply, so frankly, that the power which had been exerted over him was a power to which all Jews and all heathens might surrender themselves, because it was indeed the power of their Creator, of their God. And then, instead of considering it as a commonplace that God was the converter of Saul, and half doubting whether you must not therefore wait till some startling incident, some light from Heaven, crosses you—you will feel that this is precisely the point of contact between his life and yours; that the

eternal God is now as then holding converse
with the spirits of men; that any circumstance
which affects the body of any man, or his condition in the world, is just as really God's reminder
to him of a Presence which he has forgotten, as
the light which shone upon Saul's road to Damascus; that not the circumstance, but that
He converts men as of old. These are no
doubt anything but novelties; they have been
repeated to weariness in pulpits and in books of
devotion. But if we thought of them, if we believed them, they would surely be often mighty
helps to ourselves, great witnesses to us of our
relations to our fellow-men, a great warning to
us against the notion that any contrivances of
ours to create a sense of the Divine Presence can
bring it nearer to men than it is at every instant
of their lives. To tell them that it is nigh and not
afar off—to tell them Who would convert them,
and from what—this must be surely our task;
the more simply it is performed, the more it will
resemble his teaching who, without pomp or wisdom of words, delivered his testimony to the divine
work and will.

2. And his testimony was this, about others and
about himself—that God converts *from darkness
to light, from the dominion of Satan to His dominion.*

We cannot, I suspect, better this language. It faithfully represents what had passed and he knew had passed, within him. All his thoughts of God were of a dark being, of a being who was plotting destruction against his creatures gene- rally, who only meant to spare Jews, and among Jews only such as were faithful and resolute in maintaining the barriers that separated them from other men and in putting down all traitors within the camp. This dark being Saul worshipped. And there came to him a revelation that this was *not* the God who had said to Abraham, " In thee and thy seed shall all the families of the earth be blessed; " not the God who had said, " I am He that brought thee out of the house of bondage. Thou shalt have none other gods but Me." The God whom Saul worshipped had chosen the seed of Abraham to be a curse to all the families of the earth. The God whom Saul worshipped had not delivered him out of bondage at all. He was in bitter bondage. The very law which he was fighting for held him in bondage. It frowned at him, it cursed him. It said, " Thou shalt not covet," and it aroused in him all manner of con- cupiscence. And yet David and the Prophets had delighted in this law of God : they had medi- tated on it day and night. Saul was certainly not owning their God. And now the God of light burst upon this darkness. The Deliverer was there. The Friend of all the families of the earth was there. He was at war with Saul, for Saul hated the families of the earth. He was at war with Saul, for Saul was glorifying the Self which was his prison-house and curse, that from which only the true God could set him free. Slowly perhaps—for centuries may be crowded into such moments as these—the vision of a Father of his spirit—a Father of the spirits of all flesh— rose on him out of the night in which he had dwelt. The Lawgiver was not seeking to destroy him for his breaches of the law : He was delivering him from that spirit of covetousness which the law denounced, but which it could not overcome ; He was giving him His own spirit that he might fulfil the law.

There is much more to be said of Saul's conversion ; but if we take in thus much, have we not advanced some way towards a discovery of a sense which will be available for all times and for all men ? The man who was full of religious zeal and orthodoxy needed to be brought from the service of a dark God—in plain terms, of Satan the Adversary, the Spirit of Evil—to God. Does not every one, be he ever so religious or so

orthodox, in our days—if he is worshipping a
dark God, a God in whom he cannot *believe*, cannot trust—need conversion ?   And is not this the
tendency of us all ?   Does not our evil nature
drop easily into the acknowledgment of such a
God ?   Do we not fall into it just as Saul fell into
it ?   First, we contemplate the families of the
earth as lying outside of the church under a terrible doom; then we see the church itself exhibiting
the ugliest spectacles to the world, and begin to
ask how many of its members in any section of it
can be saved; then finally, the sense of tremendous
ghastly evil in that region which is known to each
man appals him and makes him think that God
cannot have worse designs against any heathen
or Christian than against him.   By what services,
penances, zeal in putting down the wicked, can
that sentence be averted ?   Such a state of mind
must be horrible to any whom it overtakes.
Whom may it not overtake ?   Who has not been
—nay, is not—on the edge of it ?   If any one
of us has been, at some time or other, awakened
to a belief that God is an object of trust, One
who can be loved : if that time was like a new
creation — the evening and the morning of a
first day ; the recollection may be joyful, all the
accompanying incidents of it may be worthy to

be treasured for ever; but can it be worth anything if it is *merely* a recollection, merely a date
in our existence? Was it not the opening of a
Heaven, in which the God who is the same yesterday to-day and for ever, abides? Was it not
the revelation of His purpose, His mind, to us,
when we felt ourselves the least worthy in His
universe? Was it not, therefore, the revelation
of what He is to all others as well as to us?

Surely it was thus that St. Paul contemplated
his conversion. It was a past event, but it was
the revealing of a God who is always present.
It was to *him*, but it was to him that he might
say to his own countrymen and all the outcasts of
the earth, "What God is to me, that, and no
other, He is to you." If at any time the sight
of this unchangeable brightness was clouded to
him, as he tells us that it was often—"he de-
spaired even of life; without were fightings, within
were fears"—the deliverance from that despair
was not in the remembrance of his journey to
Damascus, but in the remembrance of the God
who raiseth the dead.

And is not this the conversion which every
profligate man needs just as much as the most
religious? The sins which he has committed
have darkened the face of God to him. He dreams

6—2

of a God like himself, good-natured, tolerant of evil, so kind as to let us destroy ourselves and our neighbours without any interference, a feeble magistrate, a murderously indulgent parent. Then suddenly the features of this amiable being are changed. Under the pressure of sickness, or of some sudden calamity, he assumes the most ferocious aspect. The wrath of God—such wrath as he feels against some one who has cheated him at play, or whom he has cheated —seems settled on him. If on such a man the light breaks, if the true countenance of God shines forth—if a love which punishes the evil-doer that he may be raised out of his evil-doing, extinguishes the dream of a mercy which permits him to ruin his own soul and body, and all that are dear to him—if a burning divine wrath against that which makes us and the world wretched drives out that Devil's wrath which he had imputed to his Creator, to his Father—is this a conversion of a different kind from the other? In root and principle are they not identical?

Once more: If a man is brought out of atheism, or out of any vague conception of some power which may be malevolent or benevolent, or either by turns—which at all events is little troubled

about the world, and scarcely at all about him
one of its atoms—to the acknowledgment of such
a God as St. Paul believed in, a God whose will
is that all should be saved and come to the
knowledge of the truth, who works in the hearts
of those who confess Him that they may will
what he wills and may be His instruments in
effecting the highest deliverance for His creatures
—wherein does this conversion differ from either of
the others? What wisdom or profit is there in
using harder words towards him whom we call
an unbeliever, than towards him whom we call
our fellow-Christian? Is not unbelief the fault
of both? Is not the ground of belief, the name
and will of a God who invites belief by making
His own righteousness and faithfulness manifest to us?

But there is another lesson from Saul's conversion. If we follow his account of it we
certainly never can describe it as the exchange
of one religion for another. He did not cease
to be a Jew when he heard the voice which said,
"Why persecutest thou me?" He had never
been truly a Jew till then. It was then he began
to sympathize with the Patriarchs and Prophets
of his land: it was then he entered into their
calling: it was then he learnt to worship the God

whom they worshipped. If, therefore, we take Saul's conversion as our guide to the scriptural or divine meaning of conversion, we never can identify it with proselytism from one opinion to another. We may desire to convert a Roman Catholic from Satan to God, just as we desire to convert a Protestant from Satan to God; but we must not desire to convert him from his opinions to our opinions. We may desire to convert a Jew from darkness to light, from Satan to God; but we must not desire to convert him from his opinions to our opinions. Saul was a proselytizer *before* his conversion. He belonged to the school which compassed sea and land to make a proselyte, and which made him twofold more a child of hell than themselves. Those are dreadful words. They were not spoken by one who was passionate or ignorant; they were spoken by One whose words do not pass away. You and I have equal need to remember them.

"But how can I remember them," you may ask, "if I go forth to convert men who are heathens into Christians?" That is a subject which I shall consider in my next letter. It will bring forth another side of Saul's history: it will introduce another topic in the Bishop's speech. In the meantime, I would beseech you seriously

to examine what I have said in the light of your
own experience. You are living amidst English
colonists, as well as heathens and Mussulmans.
Are you not often troubled to know which need
conversion most ? Do you not feel at once the
great blessing of the higher ideas of justice and
truth which the colonist brings with him, and
the curse which accompanies the discovery that
he has the same propensities as the idolaters,
and that those propensities often attain as complete a dominion over him ? And then the
passions of the different sects and schools which
undertake to spread the Gospel of the West
according to their different schemes—how are
you to explain these to your catechumens or to
yourself ? The riddle is an awful one. But its
very hopelessness drives you to the old Scripture
solution. The dialect of St. Paul is the only one
you can adopt; every other must break down
with you. From darkness to light, from Satan
to God: no other description will avail you but
this. It makes your message an equally
blessed one to Europeans and to natives, to
the baptized and the unbaptized. You take
away nothing from the first: you remind them of
all the lessons which they were taught in their
infancy, of the God who adopted them to be His

children. You bid them turn to the God with
whose name they are sealed. You bid them
bear witness that He is the God of all, the God of
the earth, of the people whom they are mixing and
trading with. You say that this God is always
living, always acting upon all His creatures,
always seeking to bring them into His family.
And that message will be the most cheering to
you in your own heart as well as in your work.
Oh! the joy to read again the 23rd Psalm, as
if it told us of an actual Shepherd who does
not convert His sheep once out of their wander-
ings, but is continually bringing them back into
the path of righteousness for His name's sake!
If it is the privilege of the heathen and the unbeliever to be converted, and if the Christian or the
believer may hug himself with delight because
there is no more conversion for him, how much
better is the portion of the former than of the
latter! May you, my friend, learn more and more
that God's converting mercies to us and to mankind are new every morning. What boots it to
ask how far we have erred and strayed? If our
life is in trust, if our home is with God, we can
be right only when we are trusting, we can have
rest only in Him. Those who teach others must
know better than any how little they have trusted,

how restless they have been. They must know
better than any how often truth in the inward parts
has been exchanged for secret insincerities, tam-
perings with conscience, trifling with God. Is
it not written, " If our hearts condemn us, God
is greater than our hearts, and knoweth all
things ? " And is not that a message of comfort, a message of salvation ? What should we do
if we were left to our hearts and their condemna-
tion ? What so good as to be able, at every
moment, to say, believing that there is One who
hears, " Search me, O Lord, and try my heart,
and see if there be any wicked way in me, and
lead me in the way everlasting." If the " we "
of the Confession is said by the clergyman for
his flock, and not with them, it must soon
become an equal mockery to both. If, in our
acts of worship, we do not turn to the God of
all goodness, because He is turning us to Him,
we shall turn in those acts to the Power of Evil :
they will help to fix us in his service.—Ever
yours, &c.

LETTER VIII.

CHRIST AND ANTICHRIST.

My dear Friend,—That Saul was not converted *from* the faith of a Jew I have said already; most people, I suppose, who believe his words and reverence the Old Testament, will agree with me. But was he not converted *to* the faith of a Christian? Let us understand the question, and not be deceived by customary forms of speech.

Of course neither Saul nor any Pharisee would have allowed the name of Christians to the Nazarenes. Was not every Jew looking for the Christ—for the Son of David whom the Prophets had spoken of—for one who was to reign over the house of Israel, and before whom the nations were to bow down? Was not the great sin of the Nazarenes, in Saul's eyes, that they degraded this expectation; that they affirmed one to be the Christ who had no right to the name: one whom the leaders of the nation had decided to be a blasphemer; one whom they had deliberately given up to the Romans, for assuming to be a king? Saul did not deny a Christ at all; he charged those whom he persecuted with denying the true Christ, and setting up a false Christ.

"Yes," some one will say, "he expected a glorious Christ, when he ought to have acknowledged a suffering Christ." What! and did the vision on the way to Damascus lead him to abandon his faith in a glorious Christ? Was it not a vision of One who was glorified? Was it not the glory which blinded him? Surely his conception of the grandeur of the Messiah was not diminished by that appearance; one would suppose, from his own statement, that it was immeasurably heightened.

"Still, he began with looking for a Christ to come; he ended with confessing a Christ who had come." Certainly he did not end with *ceasing* to look for a Christ who was to be manifested hereafter. He describes himself as looking for and hasting to that manifestation. The expectation of it was his one comfort under all his troubles. He bade the churches entertain it habitually; nothing else, he assured them, would suffice for their comfort.

Was there then no change, no radical change in his belief on this subject ?   The most radical change that one can imagine : a change in his whole conception of the nature of the Christ, and of His relation to human beings : no less a change than this, that he discovered Him whom he had accounted the Antichrist to be his Lord and Master, the Son of God with power; that he discovered the image of a Christ which he had framed for himself to have the features of the Antichrist.   Such a mental revolution is indeed one which is worthy to be called a conversion. Let us study it in the Apostle ; and then see whether, in this respect also, he may not interpret all later conversions.

Saul could never hesitate about *this* question, Do we want a *King?*   Evidently that was the want which all the Prophets had expressed.   Evidently the assurance which had cheered them was that they had a King, and that He would one day be manifested.   So far, Saul going to Damascus with the High Priest's commission, and Paul preaching at Athens, were of the same mind. But *what* King would fulfil the wants which the Prophets had expressed ? *what* King did they own as the true one ? of *what* King did they desire the appearance ? *Here* is the critical de-

mand. Saul saw a Cæsar reigning over the
world. That was, it seemed, the highest throne
on which a man could sit. But it was in Rome;
the King ought to be in Jerusalem. The Cæsar
treated the chosen people as a portion of one of his
most insignificant provinces. Jehovah intended
them to rule over the nations. The Christ, His
Messiah, would come to give them that ascendency. The nations would be broken in pieces
before Him; the house of David would reign
under Him gloriously.

How much, how very much even of *this* vision
was to be accomplished, St. Paul saw afterwards.
The language of the old seers he found did not
require to be emasculated by the interpretations or
the allegories of the Elders; it was far truer in
its literal form than they were. Was their antici-
pation—that which is expressed in their words
taken literally—*this*, that a King, like the Kings
of Assyria or Babylon, a King who ruled over the
nations as they ruled, should be established in
Judæa? Was not the hope of the Prophets that
all *such* tyranny should be utterly trampled down
and beaten small under the feet of the Christ?
Was the difference to be in the *place* of government, or in the *nature* of the government? in the
persons favoured or crushed, or in the fact that

all the subjects would be treated with equal mercy and justice? This was the blessing which Israel was to confer on the world. Out of it was to come the righteous Ruler, the just and gracious King; such a King as might be, and was, the desire of all nations groaning under an accursed and devilish despotism. Now Saul did, to all intents and purposes, look for a Christ who should, in His inward character, in His moral purposes, be the counterpart of the Babylonian ruler. If a Tiberius, or a Nero, had been established in the city of David, instead of the city of Romulus—if he had deserted the temple of the Capitoline Jove for the temple which Solomon dedicated—if he had put down the *flamines*, and exalted the sons of Aaron into their places—if the sacrifices prescribed in the pontifical books were exchanged for those prescribed in the Book of Leviticus—if the chief priests and elders were consulted in any emergency instead of the augurs —that would have been the revolution which answered to the dreams of Saul's imagination. The transference of power from the Latin to the Hebrew—the capacity of avenging and destroying wrested from the one, conferred on the other— this was the object which the fervid youth, in whom were embodied and concentrated the long-ings of his sect and of the religious rulers of his land, hoped for, lived for, was ready to kill and to die for. The person who should accomplish this object would be his Christ.

And now consider the revolution which was effected in his own mind, and which he anticipated in the universe. The Apostles in Jerusalem had never for a moment altered their language. St. Peter had said, at the day of Pentecost, "The Jesus whom you have crucified is the King, the Heir of David's throne. He is exalted to reign over the house of Israel." They had foretold a great and terrible day which was approaching the house of Israel. Stephen had spoken so much more distinctly of this day, that his accusers affirmed he had blasphemed the temple and the law, and declared that Jesus would come and abolish both. Stephen showed that no one had such a sense of the grandeur of the law, and of the temple, as he had; but he did not conceal his belief that his countrymen had denied the Holy One and the Just, and preferred a murderer to Him; that they had resisted the Holy Ghost, as their fathers resisted Him; that they had received the law by the disposition of angels, and had not kept it. That this Jesus, the friend of publicans and sinners, whom they had condemned as guilty of blasphemy, was at the right hand of God—was the concluding provocation which they could not bear, which led Saul to be specially eager for his death.

And now he accepts the proclamation of the Apostles in the length and breadth of it: "We have crucified our King. Jesus is the Christ. He is at the right hand of God." How was such a revolution effected? We have the explanation from St. Paul himself. "*It pleased God,*" he says, "*to reveal His Son in me.* I had thought of a King afar off, a King who should descend some day in splendour to take His throne in some ancient palace of the city which should be prepared for Him. And lo! the King is here; the Lord of my heart and reins, claiming my trust, my submission. I have been fighting against Him; He has been fighting against me. There, in the innermost region of my being, has this battle gone on. And against whom have I been fighting? Is it against an Enemy or a Friend, a Judge or a Deliverer? Or must He not be both? Can He be my Friend if He is not the Enemy of this evil which He has found out in me? Can He be my Deliverer if he is not the Judge between me and that which is holding me captive? I have been persecuting a certain set of poor heretics; I have been hating them, and hating my kind. So doing, I have been persecuting Him; because He is the Friend of these heretics, the Friend of my kind."

Now I think all the records of conversions in Christian countries which have the strongest impress of veracity, answer strictly to this description. The man or woman reports—not in such clear words as St. Paul, with many bewilderments it may be, arising from sensible impressions—how at some time or other he or she became aware of the presence of an unseen Judge or Ruler of the thoughts and intents of the heart, of One who had a right to know them— of One whose claims had been resisted. That He should permit His child, after all this resistance, to turn to Him, to trust Him; that He should promise to guide it and be its Shepherd: this the penitent recognizes as the wonderful proof of His graciousness and forgiveness. And as this sense of graciousness and forgiveness comes distinctly home to any, the recollection of ungracious and unforgiving acts, of ungracious, unforgiving thoughts, becomes especially afflicting and appalling. These must have been especially hateful in His sight; there must be a root of bitterness in the hearts from which

7

these have proceeded. There must be a Spirit
of enmity and selfishness to which the man has
yielded subjection. If we are His subjects, will He
not plant us on another root? Will he not deliver
us from that Evil Spirit, and give us His own
Spirit? Those who are brought, in a Christian
country, to a conviction of this kind, feel that
they are then really recognizing the faith of
their fathers. They are confessing Jesus to be
the Christ. They had not doubted that there
was a Jesus who is written of in the Gospels:
they had often been haunted by the vision of a
Christ. A companion, wiser, better, at all events
stronger than themselves, some man of the age,
some figure rising out of the past in the likeness which he presented to affectionate contempo-
raries, or which is detected under the reproaches
and scorn of his enemies, becomes for a time
their Messiah. Often these honours may be
divided among many: often the image may be
changed, as the habits of the child give place to
those of the youth, of the youth to the mature man;
often the chambers of imagery may be almost
unfurnished; at last a skeleton of covetousness,
malignity, hypocrisy, may inhabit and possess
them. There were in all the previous Christs some
of the shadows which have settled into this one.

There was a light which foretold that there must
be somewhere a perfect light,—one which shines,
not on this or that clever or refined or fortunate
man, but on men. The belief that Jesus, the
friend of publicans and sinners, the stern foe of
hypocrites, the deliverer from death and hell, is
the Christ, may for a while create an indifference
to those lower forms of beauty and grace which
have been ineffectual to protect us from our
tempters and oppressors. Ultimately, if that
belief prevails and penetrates the spirit, every
dear companion, every saint and hero of the
days that are past, will be owned as having
received grace from the fulness of His grace,
light from His fountain of light. To withhold
reverence from them, will be regarded as irreve-
rence to Him. Whatever in them marred or
defiled His likeness, will be hated as proceeding
from the Spirit which He vanquished, and which
He will utterly cast out.

But what has this Christ, the Christ who was
revealed in Saul, to do with that Christ who, as
he had believed, was to enfranchise his nation and
to subdue the Gentiles ? We may make artificial
distinctions between an inward Christ and an
historical Christ, a Christ for ourselves and an
Christ for the world—so destroying both : he

could make none. Who was it that the Prophets expected would overcome the Babylonian tyranny, the Babylonian idolatry? Who was it that would appear to redeem the people whom He was punishing for their revolted and disobedient hearts, for their love of the Babylonian tyranny, the Babylonian idolatry? Who was it that would make them the head of the heathen, would enable them to fulfil the covenant with Abraham, would cause a law to go forth from Jacob that would rule the nations? Was it not the Word who came to the Prophets, who spoke by them? Was He not that King who was always with them, whom they were continually resisting, who came forth from time to time out of His place that they might confess His presence and turn themselves to Him? Strange, mystical words these,—puzzling and incomprehensible to Saul whilst he pored over the Book in which he thought he should find eternal life: hard to reconcile with his notions of that Christ who was to be; and yet ever and anon pressing upon him with a painful, terrific sense of their power and reality. And now this Word, this Son of God, was actually revealed in him! It was not the dream of a distant possible future: He was near, He was at hand. The Prophets had not dealt in fantastic allegories; they had spoken the thing as it was. This mystery was the mystery of his life, of his nation's life. The King over him was that King whose goings forth had been from old, from everlasting. The people whom He had chosen to be the witnesses of Him to all the families of the earth had, as Stephen said, resisted Him as an enemy, resisted Him in every just man who had spoken to them in His name, had now at last condemned Him, the Just One, when He had spoken to them in His Father's name.

Had He been defeated because He had been crucified? St. Paul perceived that that was the hour of His victory; that then the Jewish tyrant and the Roman tyrant were shown to be weaker than the victim: the greatest powers which men could put forth in opposition to love feebler than the power of love. That which was stronger than the malice which could inflict death, he believed had been proved to be stronger than death itself. The Resurrection (as Mr. Herman Merivale has remarked in the beautiful essay of which a visit to Malta has supplied the text,) became the habitual subject of St. Paul's preaching, although no man dwelt less on the evidence derived from miracles as interruptions of the order of the universe. The Resurrection for him

was *not* an interruption of its order, but an assertion of its order. Death was the disturber. The
living Word took the flesh and blood of men
that He might vindicate the order of creation,
and overcome that which all men felt and knew
to be its enemy.

One who had died the death of all men, One
who had risen because death could not hold Him,
such an one must be *the* Christ; no other could
answer to the name. But if He had died the
death of all men, if He had conquered the death
which holds all men, could He be proclaimed
only as the Christ or King of the Jews? Must
He not be proclaimed as the Christ or King of all
men? It was not by a laboured process of reasoning that St. Paul arrived at this conclusion.
I left out the final words of the sentence which I
quoted: "It pleased God to reveal His Son in
me, *that I might preach Him among the Gentiles.*"
He could not preach Christ among the Gentiles
till He was revealed in him. Then what else
had he to do? The Lord of his heart and reins
must be the Lord of every man's heart and reins:
if Jesus was his Lord, He was the Lord of every
Gentile. Was not that the good news which the
Jews were called out of all nations to tell all
nations? Was not this the way of putting down

idols, of putting down mortal tyranny?   "Lord,
what wilt Thou have me to do?" was his cry.
"Tell this truth to all nations," was the answer.

Sweet in the mouth, bitter in the belly, was
that answer!   It was a mighty Gospel with which
he was entrusted: woe to him if he did not
preach it!   But if this was the Christ whom he
had to preach to all nations, whither was his own
nation hasting?   What Christ were they confessing among themselves, were they preaching to
the world?   A Christ certainly; but a desire of
nations?   A friend and deliverer of the human
race?   Or exactly the reverse of this?   Was it
that they exalted the Judge above the Saviour?
Alas! they were denying the Judge, their own
Judge, Him who was at that moment separating
the chaff from the wheat in them.   Was it not
certain that the one must be gathered into his
barn, that the other must be burnt with fire
unquenchable?

With bitter sorrow, a sorrow which at times
was more than he could bear, Saul beheld that
utter downfall which the chosen witnesses of the
true King of men were preparing for themselves,
by setting up a false king, a cruel king, a deified
Cæsar, in His place.   He could not charge them
with any strange enormity; he knew how natural

was the conception of such a Christ, how he had been possessed by it, how incredible any other had seemed to him. His kinsmen after the flesh were but rushing on in the course in which he had been arrested, were but adding one and another feature to that image which he had worshipped. He could not condemn them, he could only conjure them, in the name of the God of Abraham, to turn from the false Christ to the true one; he could only look forward to a terrible day, a tremendous crisis which should reveal the two in their full and deadly conflict. He could not doubt that in the flames of his own city and temple, there would be that revelation. But neither could he doubt that the fall of that city and temple would be for the riches of the world; neither could he doubt that this blindness had only happened to his country for a time; that at last " all Israel would be saved." What divine help must he have needed to sustain him in such convictions! How continually he must have been tempted to despair for the world, for his country, for himself!

The Bishop of Oxford says that we are standing in the very same peril through which the Apostle passed; that the crisis which he saw as so near at hand in his day, is close to us in ours.

It is a fearful prediction, but I cannot dismiss it as an idle one. The more I dwell upon it, the more strong the evidence for it appears to me. I cannot gather comfort under it from the fact that in many past ages of the church the cry has gone forth, " There is the Antichrist." All these cries may have expressed a radically true, a divinely inspired conviction, though they may have rashly excluded and contradicted other convictions which were not less true; though they may have overlooked hindrances to the full manifestation of the Antichristian principle and power, which ought not to have been overlooked. Was Mahomet Antichrist ? He might be an appointed witness for a faith which those who belonged to the church were setting at nought; he might be a useful and divine scourge of its idolatry. His followers might have a faith in a living God, a Ruler of nations, which the church had exchanged for the repetition of dead formulas. But so far as he represented God to be merely a Sovereign, so far as he undermined the idea that He is a Father of the human family, so far, I conceive, he was essentially Antichristian, so far he was laying the foundation of a tyranny more complete, more terrible, ultimately more opposed to all human progress and cultivation

than any which had existed in the world before
it. Was the Pope Antichrist? He might, by
his very name, be a witness *against* the glorifica-
tion of mere sovereignty, *for* the existence of a
universal fatherhood. But just so far as he represented himself to be the universal father, just so
far as he claimed to be in himself the authorized
substitute for the Divine presence and will
amongst men, just so far the Reformers were
not unjust in describing him as emphatically the
Antichristian power, the subverter of the purpose
for which the Son of God took flesh and died
and rose and ascended to the right hand of God.
Is any Cæsar of past or of later times the Antichrist? Any Cæsar in past times or in later
times, on whom that title has been bestowed, may,
like Sennacherib or Nebuchadnezzar, have had
his commission to punish hypocritical nations, to
purge the earth of some of its corruptions. But
so far as there dwelt in him the Babylonian purpose of crushing the life of nations—the free
thought, or conscience, or will of man—so far
his intents were directly at war with the intents of Him whom we confess as the Christ.
He may not have been *the* Antichrist: he had
assuredly some of the characteristics which,
when they are separated from all that is incon-

sistent with them, all that are of celestial origin, must form the Antichrist.

There is, then, no call upon us whatever to ascertain whether this prophet, or priest, or monarch has had, or has, most of these dark features which *a* prophet, or priest, or monarch, or some combination of all three, will at last present in their perfect malignity. There is the greatest call upon each of us to ask himself whether the Christ, to whom he is doing homage, is indeed a Son of Man ? is indeed one who reveals a righteous Father to us ? is indeed a King, whose purpose is to raise and regenerate, not to destroy our race ?

I think that theological indistinctness or vagueness of which the Bishop of Oxford speaks, is never more conspicuous than when we use that name upon which the Lord's Prayer, and therefore all prayer, turns. The grand question upon which the difference between the faith of the Mahometan and of him who confesses Jesus to be the Son of God turns, is ever rising full upon us who send missionaries to convert Mahometans. Is God, to the great majority of men, really and truly a Father, or only a Sovereign ? " Of course," we answer, " He is a Father, *in a certain sense.*" Then in *what* sense ? Is the certain sense an

actual sense, or an utterly unreal sense ? Is it
only that we do not think it quite comely to part
with a venerable word, to acknowledge that we
are teaching our children a mere form of words ?
Has this Father actually revealed Himself to men
in a Son who is, as St. Paul said He was, "the
Head of every man;" in whom, as St. Paul
says, "all things were created, both things in
heaven and things in earth ?" When it pleased
God to reveal His Son in Saul that he might
preach Him among the Gentiles, was it not this
discovery which burst upon him ? Did he not
learn that there *was* a real Father in heaven, who
was claiming him, not formally, artificially, in a
certain sense, but in the most radical sense of
the word, as His child ? and this that he might
tell all men everywhere—"This Father hath sent
forth His Son, born of a woman, that He might
adopt *you* as His children ?" Does St. Paul admit
of the least severance between the truth—the
fact—which was manifested to him, and the truth
—the fact—of which he was to bear witness to
Jew, Greek, barbarian, Scythian, bond and free ?
Is not the assumption of such a severance the destruction of his whole Gospel ? And yet to make
this severance is a capital part of our divinity !
The man who perceives and confesses that God

is his Father, is taught to count *that* his distinction from his kind, not the ground of a message to his kind. God is his Father, because he
is permitted to believe and know that he is his
Father; if he did not believe it and know it, the
truth, the fact, would be otherwise! He must
teach his fellow-men that with them the truth,
the fact, *is* otherwise. They may call Him
Father—it is proper to do so; but the name does
not denote an actual relation, only the semblance
of one.

Such language was, I am sure, associated in
the minds of those who first used it with a
profound sense that to call God Father was the
greatest and most amazing privilege of human
beings. They knew how long they were in learning the worth and awfulness of the privilege,
what a new life it was to them in any measure to
lay hold of it. They heard numbers of men saying that a few drops of water sprinkled on the
face of a child conferred the unspeakable gift;
they were shocked that what was to them
so inward, should be made dependent on an
outward ceremony. A protest, a vehement protest, against the notions which had been associated with baptism in England and elsewhere,
was, I am convinced, a divine necessity: without

it, our faith and our morality would have perished together. And though it seems to me that the reaction in our day in favour of the doctrine which some of the best men of the last age denounced, has also been a divine necessity,—a witness against that notion that belief creates the fact which is believed,—I dare not pretend that this reaction in itself is the least safe or trustworthy; or that the attempts to reconcile the opposing opinions have resulted in anything but a feeble compromise from which theological clearness and practical energy suffer equally. If the baptized church is not regarded as the witness to all the families of the earth of a truth; if it claims the privilege of being sons of God as one which appertains to itself because it is separated from all the families of the earth—the church must repeat in its own experience the experience of the Jews: it must set up another Christ than Jesus, a Christ who comes to deliver a certain set of men whom He favours and who choose to believe in Him; not a Christ who takes on Him the nature of man and dies for the sins of men. And the practical test and effect of this exaltation of another Christ is, that there ceases to be any acknowledgment of a real Father over the human race. The Mahometan Sovereign is all we can dream of. For though there may

be a few who claim the privilege of being His
sons, that itself is in virtue of a mere decree, a
mere act of sovereignty; so that essentially the
God of the believer, as much as of the unbeliever,
becomes a mere Allah; and I know not whether
of such a Being Mahomet may not be the very
best prophet.

But the demand for Fatherhood will remain
deep in the hearts of human creatures after they
have enthroned a mere arbitrary ruler in the
highest Heaven. If there is no access to a Father
in Heaven, an image or counterfeit of Him on
earth will be sought after. Let no one wonder
then if men, as much now as in former days—in
Protestant countries more than in those to which
the name is familiar and in which its weakness
is made manifest—crave for such an image. The
protest against it arose from the discovery that
there *was* a way to another Father; that it had
been blocked up; that it was still open for all who
would seek it. But the father in Rome spoke of a
universal kingdom: he said that the world owed
him homage. The Reformers could only speak of
a way *for those who would seek it.* They did indeed
practically say much more, for they preached a
Gospel to sinners; their very Calvinism forced
them to say that God sought men who did not

seek Him. But as the limitation upon God's will and God's power has more and more been accepted by men of different schools—as the idea of a Sovereign for the world at large, of a Father only for the excepted few, has become the prevalent idea of Protestant divinity—the universality of the mortal fatherhood has come forth with an attraction by which a number have been overpowered, and for which they have confessed that *their* religion offered no substitute. In vain they have been told that the faith to which they are betaking themselves is an exclusive one; that it denounces all beyond the pale of the church as accursed; that it defines the church by the Popedom. They have declared that practically this system is less exclusive than the one which they desert for it; that both in space and time, both with reference to those who are in the world and those who have left the world, it is far more comprehensive. That Protestants should dread the advance of Popery when it is enforced with these arguments, addressed to some of the deepest necessities in man for which they have failed to provide, is reasonable. And *they* are equally reasonable in saying that the Popery which is accepted under such conditions will in general not be of a better, but of a far worse kind, than that which prevailed in another day. The Pope as a dogmatist will be more simply a substitute to the conscience and the reason for a Divine Teacher; the Pope as a father will stand far more practically between the worshipper and the Divine Father. I speak not of particular cases. There may be all possible modifications arising from circumstances; in many cases the new faith may be a more genuine as well as a more charitable faith than that which it supersedes. But, in general, I conceive, the Protestant who betakes himself to the Papal system will do so because the invisible world has become either incredible to him, or an intensely painful object of contemplation; because he wants something at once to suggest it to his imagination and to keep him from the perpetual terror of it. The vision of God is so vague and yet so tremendous, that he would be protected from it by intercessors and mediators, seen and unseen. The Virgin may have suggested, may still suggest, most blessed thoughts to a number of those who worship her of Divine grace and protection: God may come nigh to them in her as in any mother on whose knees they have been nursed. But she *may* become a mere form of tolerance and benignity to save the heart and conscience from the searching eye of

the Eternal Truth and Righteousness. Which she
has been to any one in any past time, which she
is to any one now, only that eye can discover.
But I cannot conceal it from myself that our way
of considering *Christ's* mediation must lead those
educated amongst us who seek her mediation to
give it the evil form and not the good. A Christ
who shields us from the God that sitteth in the
Heavens, who protects us from His fury—is not
this the Christ that is very often presented to our
imagination, I dare not say to our faith? Where
that language is not used, as it sometimes is,
formally and directly, is not there that vagueness,
that theological indistinctness of which the Bishop
complains, in our thoughts of Christ? Is He not
partly conceived of as the Son in whom the world
is reconciled to the Father, in whom men are at
one with the Father; partly as One who saves us
from the Father's wrath which, but for His interference to arrest it, would destroy us as it will
destroy the world? Is not this to confound Christ
with Antichrist, because we have first committed
the other sin to which the Bishop says we are
liable, of confounding God with the Evil Spirit?

Yes! it seems to me that if Christ is thus
needful to keep us from God, instead of bringing
us nigh to God, any number of mediators, descend-

ing to the lowest upon earth, may be needful to keep us from Him, to avert *His* wrath and vengeance. That is the Popery developing itself out of the very heart of Protestantism—defending itself by the current phrases of Protestantism—which we have a right to dread. Certainly no repetition of these Protestant phrases, no access of Protestant fury, will deliver us from it. The Bishop's remedy—a solemn examination of ourselves whether we are in very deed confessing Jesus to be the Christ—must be far more effectual.

When I speak of our dreading Christ, and asking a protection from him, I am using what may sound very fearful language; but a moment's reflection will convince you that I have a right to use it. We speak of Saul as owning a Christ who was to come, when he should have acknowledged a Christ who had come; but *we* cannot rest in the thought of a Christ that has come more than he could. We are living in an actual world, full of beauty, full of misery: what is to become of the world, must be a question with us which no conviction of any good or evil that has befallen it can set aside. Is Christ to destroy the world, or to save it? We may repeat a thousand times, "He has died to save the world;" but if when we say, "He is coming to judge the

quick and the dead," we mean by these words,
" He is coming to condemn the greater part of
the quick and the dead to utter hopeless ruin,"
we shall have an infinite dread of Christ, we
shall inspire others with an infinite dread of Him,
let our thoughts of the salvation which He once
wrought out be what they may. The fear and
horror of His appearance in glory will be the
greater for the significance which we attach to
the events of His appearance in great humility.
We shall think, " All has been done for our race
that could be done, and all has been done in vain.
Christ was once a Saviour, so far as He could be ;
now His mind and purpose have changed. He
will be manifested to take vengeance on those
who have not accepted the offer which He has
made them." I need not tell you that such is
the language of our pulpits, of those in which no
extravagant doctrine is preached, which best
represent the ordinary religious opinions of the
day. And the preachers in the pulpits actually
suppose they are entering into the spirit of that
Apostle who longed for the appearing of Christ
in glory as that which was to accomplish the
purpose of His death—which was to deliver, not
only the sons of God, but the whole travailing
creation. Surely, surely, if we believe Jesus to be

the Christ, we must believe Him to be the same
yesterday, to-day, and for ever. If we believe that
he has redeemed men by His blood, we must bid
them look for the day of His manifestation as the
day of their redemption. We must tell them that
the tyrants of the earth are to fall before its Deliverer. We are to speak of a wrath, a terrible
wrath, which will come upon the earth to purge it
of its crimes and oppressions : of a wrath which
must especially make *us* tremble, since we like the
Jews have been entrusted with a message of salvation to the world, and we like them have pretended
that it was meant for us, and that damnation
is for the world. If we do not think of these
things, if we do not ask ourselves what we have
to hope, and what we have to fear, if we do not
long for the judgment which shall bring all things
to light, we may find that we, like the Jewish
priests, have no king but Cæsar, that our Christ
is the most fearful tyrant which the world has
ever seen. And then when Jesus is revealed,
as he was when Jerusalem fell, to show who is
King of kings and Lord of lords—we, who have
sat at His feast, and taught in His streets, may be
fighting on the side of His adversary.

Oh, my friend ! help in God's strength to
keep this dire calamity from us ! You are sent out

to preach Christ to heathens and Mahometans :
therefore you are not sent out to proselytize them
to any opinion of ours. You are to proclaim
Him as the Son of God, as the Head and Friend
of every nation and every man ; therefore you are
not to leave an impression upon the minds of
any that He is our King and Deliverer more than
He is theirs. You are to tell them that He is
in you, testifying against your evils, encouraging
you to trust in His righteousness ; therefore that
He is in them, testifying against their evils, leading them to trust in His righteousness. They
have many Christs : whatever person they reverence
most, in the visible or invisible world, is their
Christ. You will say to them, Jesus who has
borne the nature of every man, who has died the
death of every man, is *the* Christ : so whatever
has been good in their old faith will be sancti-
fied and adopted into the new; whatever is foul
and dark will be renounced. You will speak of a
Father who loved the world, and sent the Son,
His express image, by whom He had formed it,
to redeem it from its enemies. You will say
that through this Son there is a way open for
them to the Father in Heaven ; that they may
seek Him, because He is seeking them. You
will not distract their minds with thoughts of

two Christs, one that has come to save, another that will come with quite another mind to judge. You will represent the judgment as the completion of the divine work of salvation. You will teach them what are the enemies from whom He came to save them, what are the enemies between whom and them He is judging now and will judge hereafter. Thus you may hope that God by your means will convert them from the Devil's Messiah to His Messiah, from him who will come in all deceitfulness and wickedness, to the Word whose purpose is to set righteousness and truth on the earth. Your battle will be with false Christs, or partly false Christs; less directly than ours with the Antichrist. But if you fight your battle bravely, you may make us understand much more clearly and fully what ours is. You may show us how our tolerance of the confusion between Christ and Antichrist is confusing your work whilst it is hastening our ruin. You may stir us up to pray, and may join with us in the prayer, that God will separate for ever between the Enemy that scatters, and Him in whom all are to be gathered in one.—Ever yours, &c.

LETTER IX.

HERESIES AND PERSECUTIONS.

My dear Friend,—Of all the words which fell from the Bishop of Oxford in the speech which has suggested these letters, none seemed to me more pregnant and profound than those which referred to persecution. We were in danger of worshipping the Devil instead of God, of putting Christ for Antichrist; when that frightful worship was established, when the Antichrist was confessed as the ruling power in the world, that would be the time of a sweeping persecution. For the spirit of infidelity, according to the Bishop, is the spirit of intolerance, if we become infidel the toleration which we have vaunted will disappear.

1 accept this statement in all its particulars. I do look upon any blessings of toleration which we possess as the fruit of a conflict with Devil-worship, with the spirit of Antichrist. I believe

all the persecution that ever has been in the world, has been a homage to the Devil, a submission to the spirit of Antichrist. The prevalence of that homage, the triumph of that spirit, must therefore be the signal for a persecution, the removal of whatever has restrained persecution. The Bishop's doctrine must be true that infidelity is the root of intolerance. The connexion between this warning and those which preceded it, is therefore very close. Nothing may assist us better in applying them than the devout consideration of this.

How naturally it links itself with the history of Saul and his conversion, I need not remind you. The expression which he is fondest of when he is describing his state before the light shone upon his eyes and into his heart, is: "I was a persecutor and injurious." His acts were obviously those of a persecutor. It was in the midst of a scheme of persecution that he was struck down. It was his persecution which the voice of Jesus declared to be at war with Him. The acts, he assures us, expressed very accurately the intention of the actor. He had not entered upon them carelessly or thoughtlessly. His whole heart was in them. He was sure they were acts of service to God: acts that were likely to recommend him to God, and to procure him the peace which he had not. And these considerations might have led us or any outside observer to choose any other name for him than that of infidel. He fully justifies the Bishop's explanation : he tells us, as I remarked before, that unbelief, a radical unbelief, was possessing him when he thought he was contending most earnestly for the traditions, the Scriptures, of the chosen race. If it was possible for the Evil Spirit so thoroughly to assume the form of an angel of light in his case—if infidelity could hide itself in him under the greatest confidence and security of belief—which of us can say that the Bishop's admonitions are not needful for him, that the test of the infidel spirit which he gives may not be the true one now as in the latter days of Jerusalem ?

Think of those latter days in relation to the history of Saul. He was persecuting to the death the sect or heresy of the Nazarenes. He himself belonged to the sect or heresy of the Pharisees. To some sect or heresy every Jew was supposed to be attached He might be a Sadducee, comparatively indifferent to forms and traditions ; he might be a Pharisee, intensely zealous for them ; he might be an Alexandrian; he might be an

Essene; he might be an Herodian. But by some name he must be described. To be simply a Jew, simply a child of Abraham, was nothing: a publican might be that, a harlot might be that. A man must have some scheme of doctrine, some rules of practice. What were they? What did he call himself? Whence did he come?

It was the leading offence of the disciple of Jesus that he did not own himself one of these sects. His Master, he said, had spoken to publicans and harlots, had treated them as children of Abraham, had said that He came as the common Shepherd of all. He had passed much of His time in Galilee; he had mixed with Samaritans. Those who called themselves His church in Jerusalem, interpreted His words and His acts as the words and acts of One who had demanded the allegiance of all as subjects of His kingdom, had put down the Spirits to whom they had surrendered their bodies and spirits. In that character the people had reverenced him: in that character the priests had accused Him of sedition before the Romans. If He was not a King, the Church had no message; if He was a King, it could not be a sect, it must be a witness of Him to the whole commonwealth.

The Apostles were therefore at war with the

sects as such : not with the Pharisee more than the
Sadducee: with both equally so far they divided the
nation which Jesus came to unite.   But Pharisees
and Sadducees both must treat them as a sect.
Their ridiculous pretension was an offence on different grounds to each: to the Pharisee because
it assailed his influence over the people, to the
Sadducee because he scorned the people.   These
sects had felt that they had a common interest
against Jesus.   Those who affirmed that He
was alive, and a King, must be described as
Nazarenes, as men who had tried to set up a
Galilean pretender on the throne of David, and
who, having failed in that object, were instituting
a new kind of doctrine in his name.

Contemplated as a doctrine, it was more disagreeable to the Sadducees than to the Pharisees.
The disciples of Jesus spoke to a spirit in man,
they spoke of a baptism by a Divine Spirit; the
resurrection of Jesus was the sign that He was
the Christ.   The Sadducees had differed from
the Pharisees in denying all communication with
the unseen world, all idea of a life after the
breath had left the body.   The Nazarenes, it
seemed to them, were reviving these tenets in a
more outrageous, and yet a more alarming form,
because one appealing to the sympathies of the

multitude. What, as the opinions of a school, were only follies, might, they thought, when thus embodied, be dangerous to the peace of society. They were in the ascendant : the High Priest was of their sect : it was needful to crush men whom they despised, when they had such an instrument for influencing the heart of an already disaffected nation.

From their more violent plans of persecution, we are told that the leader of the Pharisees in the Sanhedrim dissented. Gamaliel's party was down. He had much experience ; he had seen too many pretenders to have much dread of any new one ; he thought the new sect would fall to pieces of itself ; if it did not, it must have some divine element in it. Perhaps it might serve to keep alive some parts of the Pharisaic doctrine in the minds of the multitude ; at all events, the extinction of it would be a triumph to those who denied Angel and Spirit and the future state of rewards and punishments.

But what resemblance was there between the Pharisaical doctrine of a possible descent of an Angel or Spirit from some distant Heaven, and the Christian proclamation of a Holy Spirit actually coming from the Father of Spirits to claim outcasts as His children ? What was the resemblance between the Pharisaical doctrine of a future state of rewards and punishments, and the proclamation that One who was the Head and King of the whole nation had risen from the dead because He was mightier than Death ? When Jesus was walking on earth, He denounced the Pharisees *specially* as the foes of what was inward and spiritual. They made clean the outside of the cup and the platter, within was extortion and excess. Unless the righteousness of His disciples exceeded their righteousness, they could not enter into the Kingdom of Heaven. The whole teaching of the Apostles intimated that Christ had come to make the tree good, that the fruit might be good ; to establish them on a new root, to give them a new life. They could not separate the Resurrection from this new life : Christ had risen from the dead, that He might bestow it upon those who confessed themselves to be dead in trespasses and sins. The Resurrection did not refer to the future more than to the present : it did not concern those that were well, but those that were sick. To the man who was hugging himself with the thought of the good deeds that were to be paid for hereafter, it brought no comfort at all. However moderate, therefore, might be the temper of

some of the Pharisees towards the sect which
the Sadducees wished to put down, it was clear
that such a temper could not last very long.
The Church of Jerusalem told the Jews that
Jesus was *their* King. What if they should take
that next step which was obviously involved in
the first ? What if they should say He was the
King of *men?* What if they should say that the
chosen nation had existed to tell all nations
that their Desire, their Deliverer, had come ?
Then the Pharisee would feel that his strongest
opinion was assailed—that his sect, far more
than that of his rival, was defied. Then the zeal
which was more characteristic of him than of
the Sadducee—which was only composed in the
last of fear and contempt mingled in various
proportions—would be stirred to its depths.
Even before the Rubicon was passed by Peter's
going among the uncircumcised, the clear language of Stephen could leave no doubt whither
that which called itself the Church was tending.
It could not stop short of the proclamation that
He whom it announced as the Son of God was the
Head of every man ; and that there was in man,
in human beings, a spirit which His Spirit had
come to bring out of its prison-house, to claim as
the child of God, the inheritor of a Divine life.

The pupil of Gamaliel was not misled by any seeming likeness between the message of the Church and the notions about spirits or a Resurrection which were entertained by the Pharisees. He felt that it was a deadly war, that it behoved his school above all others to engage in the war. The High Priest, when Saul was in the fervour of his passion, was a Sadducee. It might be a humiliation in one sense to ask his help, but it was a triumph in another: it was turning the services of an enemy to account. To win such co-operation even very zealous men will stoop to mean concessions. He had no occasion for any. The Sadducee had shown himself eager enough to persecute. He might be very glad to find in the opposing ranks a man ready to undertake a commission for which few in his own would have had sufficient energy. It must have been a satisfaction that a promising disciple of the man who had rebuked his party for their violence should suggest measures so much more sweeping and exterminating than any which they had dreamed of.

Thus these two rival sects, existing in the heart of the Jewish nation, illustrated a truth which all later history was to establish—that it is the Sect temper, the Sect spirit, which, just so far as it prevails, is, and must be, persecuting, let the notions which the sect professes be what they may. And they illustrate—for us at least who receive the narrative, and acknowledge the pretensions of the Apostles to be a church—that the Spirit which has formed the Church, the Spirit of holiness, must be always at war with the Sect spirit, the Spirit of persecution. Saul, once converted, never scrupled to say, " The persecuting spirit which had dominion over me was the Evil Spirit. I was driven on by that. The Evil Spirit whom I mistook for God made me a hater of mankind. The Spirit of the Father and the Son inspires me with a love for mankind, lays on me the obligation to tell men that this love is in God Himself, and how it has been manifested."

But in every church of Jews and Gentiles which his Gospel called forth, the Sect spirit, which had once ruled him, appeared to rend and torment it. An eminent Statesman of our days once amused the House of Commons by saying that his opponents having established a Coalition Ministry seemed also to dream of a Coalition Church. Now it was just over such a church as this—the one which struck this politician as so ridiculous and incredible—that the

9

Apostles—St. Paul especially—had to watch. It
was formed from a coalition of the most unsociable
elements that ever were, or could be, combined.
The man who had grown up in a continual protest
against idolatry, who had cursed it from his infancy,
was brought into coalition with the man who had
grown up in the worship of idols, who had never
separated his thoughts of anything divine from
these, who regarded every one who tried to
separate them as an atheist. And this statement represents most feebly the difficulties of
this union. Every Jew brought with him not
only the conviction, " The Lord our God is one
God," but the habits and lessons of the opposing sects which had accepted that announcement
as divine. Every Greek brought not only with him
an idolatry, but a specific local idolatry which
might be unlike that of his neighbour. He
brought with him, besides his idolatry, the
delight in opinions, the habit of clinging to
some sophist or professor who taught opinions
opposed to those of other candidates for popular
admiration or for the favour of the enlightened
few. The Greek had given proof throughout all
history of his sectarian tendencies, of their connexion with the liveliness of his feelings and his intellect. No circumstances were so sure to develop

them as those in which he found himself in the Church.

We commonly attach great significance to what we call the peculiar gifts of the Apostles: we suppose they were specially effectual for the establishment of the church. St. Paul certainly did not dream that there was any power in these gifts to avert sectarian conflicts. All his Epistles say plainly that they were *not* averted. The Epistles not only refer to them, but are suggested by them. It is not the prudence of the Apostle, not his forbearance merely, which is called forth in his treatment of the sects and heresies in the different communities that arose at the sound of his Gospel. All his profoundest divinity, all in his teaching that has most moulded the mind of Christendom, is developed while he is pointing out the causes which threatened the unity of those bodies, in what the unity consisted, how it might be preserved. The Jewish claim to superiority over the Gentile on the ground of his Divine law, leads him to explain the use and blessing of the law as the discoverer to each man's conscience of his sin, leads him to proclaim the grand principle that Abraham and his children, as much as any Gentile, must believe in a God who justifies the ungodly. The grandeur of the covenant and the

9—2

law which proclaimed a righteous God, which
announced Him as *the* God of the whole earth,
is vindicated by the argument which overthrows
the Jewish exclusiveness, which asserts the Gentile's right to believe.   In this Epistle his own
experience of the terror of the law, which he had
condemned others for breaking and undervaluing,
mingles obviously and directly with the general
argument.   It is not really less present to his
mind when he is encountering the Corinthian disposition to make him and Apollos and Cephas the
heads of different sects and parties.   Does he for
one moment assert the Pauline sect to be better
than the Apollos or Cephas sect?   If he did, he
would be falling back into his old position as
an heretical persecutor of heresy.   That scheme
of conduct which had once seemed to him pious
and orthodox he had discovered to have its root
in unbelief: the spirit which prompted it and him
was the Devil's spirit.   And now the reason stands
out clearly before him.   Men are not united in
opinions; they are not bound together under
sophists.   Christ is the Head of a living body:
all are members of Him—members therefore of
each other.   Each has its distinct function which
no other can perform.   Each is to feel with the
other.   All are baptized with a Spirit who enables

the members to perform their different functions, who inspires them with sympathy for each other. If there was no such baptism, no such Spirit, the coalition of parts in the body was simply impossible: they must burst asunder. If there was such a Spirit, if it was the Spirit of God, if He was stronger than the Devil, then though the struggle with the heretical schismatical section in each society, in each man, would always be tremendous, the good must prevail at last, the evil must be cast out. It was probably some of those calling themselves Paulites who endeavoured to set up the idea of a spiritual resurrection against a bodily resurrection. The treatment of the subject in the fifteenth chapter connects it throughout with that principle concerning the body and the members, which had been developed. If the Head had risen, then the members of the body must rise; if the Head had not risen, they could not rise. It was not a resurrection which any one could claim as his privilege. In Adam *all* died, in Christ *all* should be made alive: the Spirit who had quickened His body would quicken them. Flesh and blood could not inherit the Kingdom of God; but that which had been sown in corruption should be raised in incorruption; that which had been sown in weakness should be raised in power.

In every case the heresy is overthrown by the
same method.   Christ Himself, the crucified and
risen Lord, is substituted for an opinion about
Him, or His death, or His resurrection.   The
actual union of men in Him is substituted for
any theory or dogma about the nature or mode of
the union.

In Galatia the coalition of Jews and Gentiles
was violently assaulted.   For Jews who had
acknowledged Jesus to be the Christ taught the
Gentiles of this Church that if they would be
saved they must come under the terms of their
covenant.   The whole Gospel was gone if this
heresy prevailed. And evidently it was prevailing.
It seemed to be sustained by the clearest testi-
monies of the Scriptures ; if the old covenant was
divine, what could set it aside ?   St. Paul turns
upon his Jewish opponents, will have no compromise with them : life and death are in the
issue.   He cuts the ground from under their feet.
He says that they are destroying their covenant :
they are making God's free promise dependent
upon a law which was given that men might be
shown their transgressions, and might cleave to
the Mediator in whom the promise was bestowed.
These Judaizers pretending to confess Jesus as
the Messiah, did not believe that He was the

Mediator in whom all God's promises were accomplished, who had fulfilled the law.   But the Messiah was the Son of God who had been sent in the fulness of the time to redeem men into their true state of sons of God, to bestow on them His free Spirit, that they might walk in the spirit and not fulfil the lusts of the flesh. Those who destroyed the liberty with which Christ had made them free, were making obedience to the law impossible.

The heresy which tormented the Ephesians was not one which arose out of indifference to spiritual power, out of denial of communications with the Unseen.   They were exposed to diviners who traded on the strong conviction that men had these powers and were capable of these communications.   Hence they were led to despise ordinary relations and practical duties.   While they were listening to such men they heard the message of the Apostle.   They were told of a Divine Spirit with which they might be baptized, a Spirit who would guide them into all Truth.   To turn from their curious arts, to burn their magical books, might be the first effect of belief in such tidings. But the tendency was there. It would soon mingle itself with the new doctrine.   Was not this Spirit one which gave them insight into the past and the

future? Did it not open to them hidden mysteries? .Did it not excuse them from mere rules
and formalities? An Aristotelian, old or modern,
would say, "This being the bias of the twig, bend
it the other way. These men are possessed with
thoughts of the Spirit. Give them the counter-
action of the Letter." St. Paul had not learnt
this wisdom. He speaks of the Spirit as unveiling
in that age a secret which had been kept hidden
from the foundation of the world. It was the
secret that the two divisions of mankind, the Jews
and the other nations, were one in Christ, and
would be gathered up in Him. This being so, he
asks for them the fullest illumination of the Spirit
that they may apprehend this truth. He prays
that He would make them know the height and
depth and length and breadth of the love of God,
which passed knowledge. On the ground of this
prayer, he builds exhortations not to thieve, not
to lie, not to let corrupt conversation proceed out
of their mouths. On the ground of it he builds
lessons for the life of husbands and wives, fathers
and children, masters and servants. For, as he
says—here more emphatically than elsewhere—
there is a perpetual battle between the Spirit of
Holiness and Light, and the powers of darkness,
of spiritual wickedness in high places, which were

ever seeking to drag them from their high estate
into corruption and ruin.

The Colossian Church, like the Ephesian, were
tempted to the opinions and practices which spring
from the belief of possible communications with the
unseen powers. What the Angels were, and
what intercourse Angels had with men, they were
curious to know. And that they might know they
had various contrivances and rules for mortifying
the flesh. Those who followed them carefully
would be capable of rising to the heights of mystical contemplation. Here was a seed of separation
and heresy that was sure to expand and mul-
tiply. The adepts would be severed from the
noviciates, those who were admitted to the divine
converse from those who were merely animal.
The animal man would become very animal
indeed; the man on the spiritual heights, who
despised him and stood aloof from him, would
often be surprised at the power of that which
he had denounced as material, would succumb to
it sometimes with secret hypocrisy, sometimes
with mad delight. Would not a prudent man
be careful to discountenance in such men all
thoughts of a hidden Christ? Would he not
lead them merely to the external history? It is
to these very Colossians that he sets forth Christ

in them as the hope of glory. He strikes at the
root of mystical self-exaltation by proclaiming
Christ as the Head of every man. Contempt of
the body, and will-worship, he denounces as hin-
dering the very object at which they aim. If they
seek the common Lord, Him who is at the right
hand of God—if they set their affections on Him
—that will mortify the corrupt affections, which
ascetical devices often stimulate and vivify. And
here again the plainest, vulgarest morality is
shown to be the fruit and blessing of the Spirit's
government.

The persecutions of their Jewish enemies,
the thought of their leaders' imprisonment, had
evidently produced much despondency in the
Philippians. Such despondency may be as fatal
to fellowship as self-confidence. It is strikingly
characteristic of the Epistle to them that it continually turns them from self-contemplation to the
common object, to Him who, being in the form of
God, humbled Himself, and became of no reputation, and died the death of the Cross: to Him
who is highly exalted, at whose name every knee
is to bow—of things in heaven, and things in
earth, and things under the earth. All troubles,
whether they befal the flock or its Shepherd, are
goads to him and to them, forcing them to seek

that righteousness which is not their own; which is of God; which all alike may inherit by faith. Nowhere does this high theology more associate itself with the vexations and trials of existence, nowhere do we see more how it loses its virtue for each individual man, if it is not presented to a whole body, if any line is to be drawn between those who may and may not claim the blessing of it. Such distinctions are the destruction of a church, the cause of all heresies.

Look, again, at the Epistle to the Thessalonians. They have been tormented with thoughts of some great judgment which is to overtake the nations, but especially the chosen nation. They tremble as they anticipate this judgment, this end of the world. What use is there in doing any work if the event is so nigh? why be at pains about anything? So argue these well-disposed, kindly Macedonians, who have listened to the Apostle with great earnestness—who at his word have turned from idols to serve the living and true God—who think that he has given them warnings which they are obeying in the simplest way. And has he not given them these warnings? Does he not expect this judgment? Assuredly he does. He looks for a revelation of the Man of Sin

who is opposed to the true Christ. All this, he
says, is nigh at hand. There will be a delay
before it comes. He that lets will let till
he be taken away. But the delay cannot be
long. There will be flaming fire; there will be
a sentence on those who will not have deliverance for themselves, and will keep others from it.
The old world will pass away; the Son of Man
will be revealed. These words I have partly
considered already. A new light is thrown upon
them when we recollect what St. Paul had discovered to be the curse of his nation, what he
had discovered to be the curse of all nations and
all churches. There was a time when he had
longed earnestly for the overthrow of the Roman
power, for the independence of Judæa. That was
the time when he was wishing for a Christ who
should be another Cæsar, who should merely
exalt the Hebrew and depress the Latin. Now
he perceives that the Roman power had been a
divine let or hindrance to the full manifestation
of the Antichristian Spirit. When that was no
longer dominant in Jerusalem, the Sect demon,
kept in a certain check by his justice, would
burst forth unrestrained; Pharisees and Sadducees would fly at each other's throats. The
commonwealth, long rent by them, would be

dismembered utterly. The most tremendous sentence ever passed upon a nation would be executed by its own hand. The victory of Titus would be a witness of the divine mercy, in putting an end to the religious fury. But was this a reason for the Thessalonians to abstain from work? Was this passing away of an old age— this opening of the new age, something which should shake their constancy? Was it not a confirmation of all that they had believed? Was it not a proof that they had not followed a cunningly devised fable when they had confessed the Crucified Man to be the Lord of all. Away then with this cowardice! Let each mind his own business, and do his work quietly. If he will not work, neither let him eat.

Now supposing these Epistles were intended, —as we have all said that they were—to be guides to the Church in all the stages of its history, warnings of the perils to which it would be exposed at one time as much as another, divine illuminations as to the method of escaping those perils, and of maintaing its existence, we cannot doubt (1) that sects and heresies of the most opposite kinds would spring up in every part of it, would take their shape and colour from various local circumstances, would be always

seeking to sever one portion of it from the rest.
(2.) That to set up one of these heresies against
the other, is the natural tendency of every
man.   (3.) That whoever indulges that natural
tendency assists the growth of heresy as such
while he labours to confute a particular heresy.
(4.) That every Church which should attempt to
suppress the positive opinion or conviction of any
of its members, must favour the growth of heresy
within it, and the establishment of heresy without it.   (5.) That every Church which takes
this course is likely at last to fall into the
radical heresy of denying that Christ is the
Head of a living body in which His Spirit is seeking to cultivate the thought, belief, practical
energy of each member of the body to the
utmost, and to bring the thoughts, beliefs, practical energies of all the members into harmony.
(6.) That if this heresy is fully developed, the
Church must fall into the same condition as the
Jewish nation when it yielded itself utterly and
absolutely to the spirit of division, and when it
said anathema to the Spirit of Jesus.

If this be so, our fathers were not abetting
heresy or establishing heresy when they protested
against the claim of the Papacy to put down
heresy, and to maintain the faith once delivered

to the saints. They were protesting against an heretical experiment, an experiment which had divided Christendom within itself, an experiment which had continually restrained the work of the Spirit in communities and in individuals, and which had issued in the denial of Christ as the actual and present Head of the Church and of mankind. Such a protest was a protest on behalf of a Catholic Church, a Church of Christ, a Church governed by a Holy Spirit. The protest was opposed by an appeal to numbers and to tradition, just as the testimony of the early Church was: it was resisted like that, by outward persecution. Whoever yields to this argument from numbers and tradition, ought to abhor the acts of the early Church; whoever thinks that persecution for Christian orthodoxy is justifiable, cannot in his heart and reason dislike Saul's persecution on behalf of the Jewish orthodoxy. The Pagan traditions went back as far as the mediæval traditions; the one were not more variable and uncertain than the other. Saul had far greater excuse from Scripture for treating as heretics and blasphemers those who were likely to destroy the distinction between the circumcised and the uncircumcised, than the Popes had for any one of the imprisonments and tortures which they sanctioned. I say *any one*. I would not insult the young Pharisee by comparing his worst acts with those of men who notoriously were plotting for their own aggrandisement, or that of nephews and sons, under the pretext of advancing the cause of the Church. I take the very best and most conscientious Christian persecutor whose name and acts have come down to us, and I mean that it will be hard to make out a defence for him which will not apply *à fortiori* to him who took the journey to Damascus.

But if I defend Protestants on this ground, I am bound to ask what better apology they have for any one of the persecutions by which they have endeavoured to extirpate the *belief* of Romanists, or of any sect among themselves? If they deny the right of Latins to establish a system which excludes Greeks or Protestants from the body of Christ, how dare *they* exclude Latins or Greeks, or any man of any profession whatever from His body? This surely is Protestant heresy; this is putting a Protestant opinion, a notion of ours, or a denial of other men's notions and opinions, in place of the Son of God. And such heresy has been punished, must be punished by the multiplication of heresies. Protestants began with asserting men's right to believe, not implicitly, but directly, in Christ. Such a claim necessarily awakened a multitude of thoughts which had been asleep. As they started up, half-bewildered, out of the midst of dreams, they could but assume partial, often grotesque shapes. By doing justice to each of them, by recognizing each as an effort to grasp some part of the truth as it is in Jesus, by urging all to seek for that Spirit of love and power and a sound mind, who would bring crude thoughts to maturity, irregular and disjointed speculations into unity, these one-sided efforts of earnest minds might have been saved from passing into denials and contradictions of each other; the unity of the Church might have been saved. But Protestants darted savagely at the weak point—or what seemed to be the weak point—in the statements of any one who was strongly possessed by a belief. He was accused of rebelling against the God whom he knew that he wished to serve, of rejecting the Christ in whom he knew that he was trying to trust. The possible consequences of his opinion were accurately pointed out. Young men were warned to avoid him. Many of them being earnest, and not caring for the judgment of the public, were

10

attracted to him, for he had met some craving in their minds. A school gathered about him. It fulfilled some of the predictions which had been launched forth against its founder: for it began to dwell much on his denials, on that wherein he opposed other men's faith. It was kept alive, even kept in a condition of moderate health, though mixed with symptoms of disease, by persecution. When that ceased, it stood forth the respectable, recognized sect, full of worldly precautions for the protection of its own existence, of schemes for winning proselytes from other sects; tolerant while it was apathetic, fierce in any moment of renovated vigour.

This process has been going forward in Protestant lands ever since the Reformation; the principle which has been at work in it is active in England at the present day. We have all seen the operation of it against persons suspected of Romanism, Antinomianism, Unitarianism, Hegelism, Comteism. It has recruited the ranks of each one of the schools to which these names are attached. It has turned affection into suspicion, sympathies to antipathies, convictions to contradictions. Well may the Bishop of Oxford say that our toleration is a very weak plant; a single night blast may wither it. If we do not learn to be intolerant of the Spirit of enmity and hatred who is seeking to possess us all : if we do not own that every act and thought of bitterness, by whomsoever perpetrated and entertained, is of his inspiration : if we do not own that every right thought and just work and good desire, in whomsoever it dwells, comes from the Holy Spirit : if we do not trace all tenderness and charity to Him, and remember that they are only kept alive in us or in any man by His presence : we may find ourselves, before we are aware, in the midst of that persecution which the Bishop has foretold, and alas! not in the character of the persecuted whom Jesus has blessed, but of the persecutors who are under His woe.

My friend, are not you wearied and tormented when you hear us talking to each other at home of our 'unhappy divisions?' Are not you inclined often to say, "Unhappy! what then, are they sold, as the Jews said they were, to work iniquity? Are they *fated* to do that which makes the Gospel appear an utter lie to the nations among whom it is to be preached? Is God to be charged with their evil?"

I wish you would fairly set these thoughts before you; if you do, you may preach repentance to us, you may call upon us to be converted.

10—2

The fact is this.   We have talked about the sins
of churchmen as if they were venial sins; about
the sins of men outside the church as if they were
mortal sins.   We have not frankly acknowledged
that these heresies and divisions of ours are the
root-sins of human society; those which are
threatening its dissolution; those which are most
directly at war with the Spirit of holiness.   If the
Sermon on the Mount is true, Christ did not come
to put down murder, but the hatred which pro-
duces murder; not adultery, but the lusts which
produce adultery.   He came to regenerate the
principle, not to improve the surface of human
existence.   If there is a church on earth, it is a
witness of this truth; it is a witness for the
renovation of the springs of human action.   And
the chosen witness exhibits the principle of hatred,
of separation, in its most terrible forms.

This may be a confession which we are very
slow to make, but God demands it of us; there
can be no real extirpation of Devil-worship till we
own where it begins, how it is sustained.   It was
not in the Roman power that the Apostles recognized the great foe to the Gospel; it was the
Jewish sects, those which professed most orthodoxy, that resisted the message of a restoring
Spirit.   The sects wanted to be rid of the Romans,

and to have a power like theirs. The yoke was thrown off: then began the reign of anarchy and devilry. Is it not so now? The Church desires to contend with the world. How? By proclaiming a Divine Spirit capable of working out the inward change, which no outward machinery can effect? Not at all; but by obtaining an outward machinery, which shall be a rival to the machinery of States. Such a machinery may be called a church machinery, or what you please; it will be to all intents and purposes a sect machinery; it will be a machinery for punishing heresy and for spreading heresy; it will make the Church more and more into a mortal scheme for propagating opinions, less and less into a divine society for propagating a Gospel. In fact there will be no Gospel to mankind. The Church will simply bear this message to the universe: "We are saved, you are lost." And such a salvation will not mean a salvation from any of the evil habits of the world, from pride, malice, uncharitableness. It will mean an adoption into the chosen body of all the corruptions against which it is sent to protest.

But if, utterly discarding this dream of a church, you maintain your own position as one sent out from the Church in England to tes-

tify of the redemption of the world in Christ, for
the power of His Spirit, what an example you
may set us! You wish to be a Protestant; you
will be so in the strictest sense of the word. You
will protest, not in word but act, against all
attempts to narrow the Church by setting up any
head over it except Christ. In act, I say, "not in
word," meaning that the resolution to do this will
involve no attack, open or covert, upon Romanists—rather an intense desire to claim them as
members of the same catholic fellowship with yourself. *In word*, however, emphatically in this sense:
that all your words to your heathen brethren will
be an announcement that there is such a church,
such a family, united in the great Elder Brother,
admitting men of all races and of all notions, if
they do not make their races or their notions an
excuse for separation from each other. You wish
to be an English priest: and you will be so.
You will maintain the best habits and traditions
of your country, which have neither been Romish
nor anti-Romish—which have been practical, not
dogmatic — which have recognized the State
minister as having a different function from the
ecclesiastical minister, but as not less a servant
of God. You will only throw off the narrow,
negative English tradition which interferes with

the full recognition of men as men, with the acknowledgment of their particular modes and habits as not less suitable to them than ours are to us, as being under the cultivation of the same Divine Spirit. So you will in your work illustrate the true toleration and the true intolerance—the toleration of that Apostle who became all things to all men that he might gain some; the intolerance of that heretical and persecuting temper which is the greatest sign of unbelief in God, the most acceptable of all sacrifices to the Devil.—Yours, &c.

LETTER X.

SACRIFICES TO GOD AND TO THE EVIL SPIRIT.

My dear Friend,—You will not, I hope, suspect me of using the phrase with which I concluded my last letter in any loose rhetorical sense. When I spoke of sacrifices to the Devil, I meant Sacrifices to the Devil. I do believe that we are in danger of presenting such sacrifices, of making ourselves the sacrifices.

The expression will at once recall words which are attributed in our translation to St. Paul. *"What say I then? That the idol is anything, or that what is offered in sacrifice to idols is anything? But I say that those things which the Gentiles sacrifice, they sacrifice to Devils and not to God. And I would not that you should have fellowship with Devils."* I need not tell you that this version is inaccurate, mischievously inaccurate. St. Paul says nothing about the Gentiles which they would not have admitted, nothing in the least vitupera-

tive. The demons or secondary powers presiding
over different parts of Nature, over different cities,
over favoured men, were notoriously, confessedly,
the chief objects of their worship ; to them chiefly
the sacrifices were presented. There was a
supreme God above or beneath all these demons.
He might sometimes be contemplated as Zeus,
especially when there were dreams of an earlier,
happier world which some elder, more paternal
deity ruled ; especially when some name must be
found for one who quelled the brute ambition of
the Titans or who crushed the benevolent purposes
of Prometheus towards man. But Zeus was himself full of earthly passions, which affected his
justice and determined the exercises of his power.
His could not be the all-prevailing will. He must
have had an origin. There must be something
behind him. Was it destiny ? Was it love ?
Should it be recognized as the Unknown God to
whom an altar might be raised in some great.
calamity, after the gods to whom names had
been given were exhausted ?

Most exactly then, in conformity with evident
facts, did the Apostle speak when he said that
the sacrifices were not offered to *the* God, the
righteous God whom he reverenced as the Creator
of heaven and earth, of all things visible and

invisible; but to demons which had a limited dominion in earth, or sea, and air, to whom their worshippers imputed a mixture of qualities like their own, not wholly evil, not wholly good, just such as a creature in whom a spirit was lusting against a flesh and a flesh against a spirit, would naturally create for himself. He came to withdraw the Corinthians and idolaters from such demons. He did not count the idol itself, the wood and stone which was worshipped, anything evil; he did not recognize any evil in the animal which was offered to the idol. But there was a mixed deity, made in the likeness of men, to which the worshipper did homage through the wood and stone, with which his spirit held fellowship in the act of sacrifice. Such reverence, such fellowship, were not elevating, but depraving, to creatures made in the likeness of the Eternal God. The Apostle who asserted for them the right to call themselves sons of God in Christ, would lead them from the reverence of that which, at its very best, was imperfect, which might be unclean, to the reverence of the Perfect, of the absolutely Holy; from fellowship with images of their own characters, to fellowship with Him who had shown forth His true image in His incarnate Son.

The error which identifies those demons with

powers essentially and altogether evil has not
been an innocent one. It has been the parent
of a multitude of misconceptions concerning the
Greek as well as the Hindu mythology which
have perplexed classical and oriental interpreters,
and have produced a violent revulsion in them
against the preaching of the Gospel. They have
said boldly and honestly, " Apollo, Pallas, Ar-
temis, Brahma, Vishnu, were not Devils, as
you report them to have been. There is in
them an acknowledgment of light, wisdom,
purity, which cannot be devilish." Still more
has this language confused the practice of Christian men. It was clear that the evils which
were found in Heathendom all existed in
Christendom. The names might be gone; the
powers remained. Why should not any part
of nature be in possession of some evil spirit?
Why should not any man be able to cast an
evil eye on his fellow-creatures and to blast his
fortunes or his character? Mr. Leckey has not
exaggerated the number or the frightfulness of the
crimes which thoughts and feelings of this kind
have generated in Christendom. They are some
of the more startling and tremendous phenomena in the world's history. He has done well
to fix our attention upon them, whether he has

shown us the way of deliverance from them or not.

But there is in this very mistake a singular instinct of the truth. St. Paul did unquestionably feel that his warfare was against Evil—Evil in its most radical and concentrated form. The demons whom the Gentiles worshipped were not Devils. This notion that any part of creation could be evil, was precisely the one against which he protests in the passage which I have quoted. Yet men had an inclination to worship evil: it was an inclination which was waxing stronger and stronger in that time: all the abominations of the empire were nourishing it; all the scepticism and despair about any good which could overcome those abominations nourished it. The powers of nature were assuming in men's eyes a more and more malignant aspect: the sense of any divine Kings who might appear to help patriots in their battles for freedom was waxing feebler and feebler. It was not in heathen lands, however, as we have seen already, that St. Paul discovered the centre of the conflict with spiritual wickedness. That, he perceived with awe, was in his own land; in the Temple wherein the sons of Levi still offered the morning and evening sacrifice, incense was ascending in very deed to the Devil, and not to God.

If he believed Jesus to be the Son of God
must he not have thought this? Were not the
priests, the sons of Aaron, the very men who
had cried out, and invited the people to cry out,
" *Let Him be crucified?* " Had not they refused
to enter the judgment hall, lest they should be
polluted when they ate the passover? Had not
they come from the Temple and the feast to wag
their heads and say, " *He saved others; Himself
He cannot save?* " These men represented the
hierarchy, which we all admit could claim a
divine appointment, could allege a clear succes-
sion. When had Pilate, the Roman Governor—
when had any heathen priest—exhibited an ab-
horrence of the Divine Image which could compare
with this? " *They have seen and hated both Me
and My Father,* " was the language of Jesus Himself.

With such examples before our eyes, which of
us can depend upon any felicity of position to
keep him from the abyss into which these priests
fell? Who should fear so much as those who
bear the name of priests, that their sacrifices may
be offered to the Spirit of evil instead of to the
Father of light? Which of us should not be
thankful if the stern words of the Bishop of
Oxford have recalled him to the possibility of

such an inversion of all worship, not in some other day, but in our own?

When I use this language I accept what I presume would be the teaching of the Bishop about the Presbyter of the new economy; I depart from the teaching of many whose intentions I respect and honour. I think that we, as much as any Aaronic priest, are conversant with sacrifice; that our functions and his *can* be compared. Instead of fearing to associate prayer and worship with sacrifice, I feel more and more how much my mind has suffered from the habit of separating them; how necessary it is to remember that every man—Jew, Turk, Christian, Infidel — must offer a sacrifice to some God; no less a sacrifice than himself. How grand the privilege is of being taught to *what* God we have a right to offer ourselves as sacrifices! If I did not hold that a Presbyter of the Christian Church might offer his congregation and himself as acceptable offerings to the true God, I should consider that the fewer litanies he repeated the better; that he ought never to take part in the Holy Communion.

In our Communion Service we speak of a full, perfect, and sufficient sacrifice, oblation, and satisfaction, which has been made for the sins of the whole world.   In our Communion Service we speak of offering our bodies and souls to God. Are these real or unreal words ?   What do they mean ?   Where can we learn what this full and perfect sacrifice is, to whom it has been offered, why we should give thanks for it, why our communion is grounded upon it, what it has to do with our sacrifices ?   Where can we learn in what relation this sacrifice and our sacrifice stand to those which have been presented at the door of the tabernacle by the priests of the house of Levi ?   We want information upon these subjects.   All Christendom wants it.   We cannot get it from the traditions of Romanists or of Protestants ; it is required especially that we may understand those traditions, that we may not be the victims of them.   Most persons who adhere to the maxims of the Reformation would say that we must turn to the New Testament for this help ; few will dispute that if it is to be found anywhere, it will be found in the Epistle to the Hebrews.

Among the Epistles of St. Paul, to which I referred in my last letter, I did not include that which so many in former days, and a majority of critics in our own day, have denied to be his. Their arguments may not seem to me conclusive :

the facts on which the arguments are grounded I
should insist on as much as they can. I may
not feel sure that the Apostle, whose characteristic
it was that he became all things to all men, must
have adopted the same forms of thought and
modes of expression in writing to his own countrymen, which were most suitable in addressing the
inhabitants of Gentile cities. I may not see anything very puzzling in the fact that the subject of
Sacrifice, which is only handled incidentally elsewhere, should have been reserved for special and
elaborate treatment, when he was appealing to
the conscience of men who prized sacrifices
which he and they acknowledged to be of divine
appointment. That the Epistle is not essentially,
vehemently, Pauline in *this* sense, that it is occupied throughout with a protest against a relapse
into the conditions of the old covenant—no
commentator, however learned, can persuade me.
But we owe the deepest thanks to those who have
forced us to notice the peculiar structure of this
book, who have not allowed us to confound it with
others which have a quite distinct character and
purpose. Such observations are real helps to the
right understanding of the Epistle; and that is
what we require. I hold this Letter to be the
one which most discovers to us our dangers at

this time, and may most clearly point the way out of them. The dispute about authorship may entertain those who have leisure for it; the meaning of the Epistle is a question of business for us and for our children.

I will draw your attention to some of its most obvious features. You will of course compare the words with the text, to see whether I have perverted it.

He affirms—I. That God is speaking to men through a Son who is the express image of His Person, by whom He made the worlds. II. That such a Son is spoken of by the Psalmists and Prophets of the Old Testament; that they recognize Him as above all Angels, as one with the Eternal God, as the Brother of suffering creatures on earth. III. That because those of whom He was the Brother were partakers of flesh and blood, He also took part of the same; that He was made lower than the Angels for the suffering of death; that He had tasted death for every man: that He had been crowned with glory and honour; that so were fulfilled the words of the Psalmist, which declared that all creatures, according to God's original law, were subject to man. IV. That this suffering and exalted Son is the High Priest, the perfect Mediator between God and

11

man, not in virtue of an arbitrary decree, but of an
eternal constitution. V. That priests on earth
—being appointed by a mere decree however
divine a decree—could not fulfil the meaning of
the priesthood, which implied the perfect union
between the worshipper and the object of worship.
VI. That the sacrifices of the Jewish law being
animal—being sacrifices of something belonging to
the person, not of the person himself—could never
satisfy the demands of the conscience for reconciliation with God. VII. That the outpouring of
the blood of animals, which was appointed by the
Jewish law, could never purify the conscience from
its defilements. VIII. That the sacrifice of Jesus,
because it was grounded on a perfect union of the
will of God and the *will* of the Man, did satisfy
the demand of the conscience for reconciliation.
IX. That the pouring out of *His* life-blood did
take away the conscience of sins. X. That on
this perfect mediation, this perfect sacrifice, rested
a new covenant which had superseded the old,
this being the tenour of that covenant : " *I will
write my laws in their hearts, and in their mind
will I write them ; and I will be their God, and
they shall be my people, and their sins and iniquities
will I remember no more.*" XI. That the blessedness of this mediation and sacrifice was that men

could draw nigh to God with pure hearts and clear consciences, entering, not into His figurative, but His actual presence, in Him who had withdrawn the veil from the Divine countenance, in whom men might know that they were reconciled to their heavenly Father. XII. That the Church of Palestine and the Hebrew Christians, generally, through trust in sacrifices which could not take away sins, in carnal ordinances which were soon to be swept away, were sinking into practical unbelief. XIII. That an earthquake was at hand which would shake, not earth only, but also heaven ; and that if they were trusting in any outward economy, not in Him who had established it, and of whose divine purposes it bore witness, they would be found apostates. XIV. That this same crisis would reveal the God who had been the object of faith to all past generations. The men whose names they reverenced most had subdued kingdoms, wrought righteousness, turned to flight the armies of the aliens because they believed in a God who was a living Deliverer, and who would reveal Himself more perfectly to their descendants than to them. XV. These witnesses were about them now; if they entered into their faith, if they believed in Him who had fulfilled the expectation of their fathers, they would have fellowship with an innumerable company, with the Church of the First-born, with God the Judge of all, with the Mediator of the New Covenant, with that blood which spoke of reconciliation between brothers as the blood of Abel spoke of their separation. XVI. Remembering this reconciliation, they could keep alive brotherly kindness, hospitality to strangers, the purity of the marriage bed, compassion to the afflicted. These were acceptable sacrifices, which those could offer who did not stand in the outer tabernacle, but who might approach the highest altar. If they claimed that privilege, they might be content to bear reproaches. Christ had borne all reproaches : He had suffered without the camp before He went into the Holiest of the Holies.

These lessons, by whomsoever they were first written down, interpret the very existence of Christendom, the meaning of that Eucharist which was regarded as the highest act of worship, as the celebration of the highest sacrifice, as the participation in it, as the witness to all men of Christ's death till He should come, as the offering of men's bodies, souls, and spirits to the Eternal God that He might work in them to will and to do of His good pleasure. In this sense the Eucharist subverted the sacrifice to demons ; in this sense it asserted the privilege of men, through their union in the Son of Man, to rise above the service of Angels, and claim fellowship with the Father of all.

The Reformers in the sixteenth century discovered how little the sacrifice which was celebrated daily in the cities of Christendom bore this witness, how much it bore an opposite witness. It spoke of a redemption and atonement, not accomplished once for all by the High Priest, but to be accomplished by priests on earth; not of a communion with Him who was within the Veil, but of a figurative heaven brought down to earth. It delivered men from no demon-worship. It threw them upon demon-worship. The highest heaven was still behind the Veil. God had descended into the elements. Yet even in that form, only the priests might approach Him: the people must seek intermediate intercessors. Saints, some derived from the past, some dwelling in local spots and commanding local blessings—all imperfect, preferred for their imperfection, adapting themselves to individual tempers and diseases, must defend them from the Judge of all. Dead relics were to hold those bound, who professed to believe in a risen Christ.

Here was a ground for noble protests. The

words " finished salvation " became the watch-words of the Reformation. Cries against the Mass as a denial of the Mediator and of His atonement, resounded from the pulpits of Protestant divines, often led to outrages against the existing form of worship in countries where Protestantism had obtained ascendency, and where, through its rulers or its mobs, it could return some of the persecutions which it had undergone.

But it was to give its opponents *their* revenge. The common Mass was exchanged for prayers or sermons, or a mixture of the two, in Protestant churches; but where was the pledge of a finished salvation? Where were the signs to the world that any communion had been established between men and God, because He who was the perfect image of God had taken the nature of man, and had died the death of man? Where was the thanksgiving for such a reconciliation? Where was the assurance of all those blessings which the Epistle to the Hebrews declares that the Son of God had claimed for the race, and the forgetfulness of which, in those to whom he wrote, he counted a token of coming apostasy? The Communion offers a badge to each of the sects into which Christendom is divided. But since the idea of sacrifice can never

be banished from any society of men, since the
name Atonement is felt to express the characteristic of a Christian community, it must be
explained *why* an atonement has been necessary,
why it should be connected with sacrifice.   The
explanation is just that which a heathen would
offer:—Men have sinned against the highest God ;
He must have recompence or satisfaction for their
sin.   If He pardons any, some adequate price
must be found for His pardon.   Christ has offered
this adequate price.   God may now forgive the
offences of His creatures—of those at least who
understand and accept this scheme of salvation.

God forbid that I should say this was the *faith*
of our nation, or of any nation.   Where there is
anything like a Lord's Supper, however it may
have been changed into a symbol of party and
division—where the Epistle to the Hebrews is read
and accepted as a divine document—where such a
conscience has been awakened in men as a Gospel
recognized, however imperfectly, for one thousand
years must awaken—wherever a faint echo of the
voice that shook Christendom out of its slumbers
in the sixteenth century still lingers among us,—
there it is impossible that a scheme of salvation
should ever entirely displace an actual salvation ;
that the High Priest and Mediator who unites

men to God, should be exchanged for a Mediator who interposes to shield men from God. But the most opposing influences are leading us to this result. The Unitarians as a sect have declared that the ideas of propitiation, atonement, sacrifice, belong to a barbarous theology; that the simple worship of a Father in Heaven excludes them; that prayers may be constructed without the least reference to them. Numbers who have no special sympathy with the Unitarian sect, yet observing the effect of notions about sacrifice upon both the heathen and the Christian world, have eagerly joined in this protest, affirming that it was good for the interest of civilization, let its divinity be worth little or much. On the other hand, men who have felt the demand for sacrifice and atonement in their inmost hearts, who have been certain that the rites practised by all kindreds of the earth inarticulately express this demand, have resolved that they would not purchase the reputation of being civilized, or of having an amiable, reasonable theology, at the price of being dishonest to their own convictions or of separating themselves from their fellow-creatures. Such men, when pressed by arguments which they cannot answer, naturally turn to the explanations of sacrifice which apologists and divines supply; persuade themselves that these are the necessary protections against the Unitarian denials; and so endorse, for the sake of controversy and confutation, a theory which in hours of bodily anguish and spiritual conflict proves incapable of sustaining their hope for others or themselves.

Meantime the more learned Unitarians, convinced that the ideas of sacrifice and atonement which they had wished to eliminate from the New Testament occupy a very prominent place in it, have learnt to treat its different books in the spirit of modern criticism, attributing them to Alexandrian mystics or schoolmen who were bent upon constructing a theological or theosophical theory. It is very important for this purpose that they should insist upon the ordinary popular representation of these books as the only true one. They therefore fraternise eagerly with the orthodox critics, if in nothing else, yet in their expressions of scorn for those who complain of their interpretations. " Of course," they say, " the only natural sense of the doctrine is the common one. Those who think otherwise, are trying to reconcile the notions they have learnt from later times with a superstitious reverence for the book. Either from self-interest or from the

impulse of an irregular and insane fancy, they
wish to make both the fishermen and the doctors
speak the dialect of the nineteenth century."
Such censures are caught up triumphantly by
their opponents. "We need not argue," they
say, "with those who pretend that our notions
of sacrifice are not the notions of the Apostles.
The Unitarians and Rationalists decide that
question in our favour."

Such a consensus of opinions is of course very
formidable. And there is a more formidable consensus still. Protestants and Romanists, even while
they denounce and excommunicate each other,
yet appear to recognize the fact of depravity, of
Evil, as the fundamental fact of divinity. The fall
of Adam—not the union of the Father and the
Son, not the creation of the world in Christ—is
set before men in both divisions of Christendom
as practically the ground of their creed. The
teachings of the Divine Word—whose delights
were with the sons of men, who was the Light of
the world—if they are recognized at all, are only
spoken of as disturbances of an all but unbroken
devilry: the incarnation itself, the death of Jesus,
the resurrection of Jesus, are but events which in
some small degree, for some portion of the world,
diminish the victory of the Destroyer: for men in

general they make that victory more appalling and
more secure.   The general Mass, therefore, of
the Romanist nations, the public worship of the
Protestant nations, can but present themselves to
the body of the citizens in both as needful though
very feeble protections against a Power which is
threatening them with ruin, and which may possibly be soothed and caressed into pity.   Is not
this to make our sacrifices Devil-sacrifices ?   Is
the warning of the Bishop needless, that we should
one and all see whither our theological indistinctness is leading us—in what a worship it may at
last issue ?

And yet I believe a reformation more complete
by far than that of the sixteenth century may be
awaiting us, through the mercy of Him whom we
have reviled.   I do not expect it to come merely
through the study of the Epistle to the Hebrews,
or of any portion of Scripture.   In Luther's day
the Bible did not come first.   Bitter anguish came
first: the Bible spoke to that.   I do not expect
it to come from creeds or sacraments : they
correspond like the Scripture to human necessities.   When we are not awakened to a sense of
these, creeds and sacraments may be to us—what
they are now.   But if there should go forth a
message even from the feeblest lips, " God is

verily the Atoner, the Reconciler of human beings.
He has made them one in Christ. He has made
peace with ·them in Christ. The Divider has
proved weaker than the Uniter. The Son who
could give up Himself to do His Father's will has
prevailed over the Spirit of self-will, to which we
have all yielded "—then we may leave the Unitarian critics to do their worst against the book
which testifies of this Atoner, of this offering.
They may prove their critical point to their own
entire satisfaction—who will care? If the book
speaks to that which I and they have need of—it
may have been picked out of a ditch, it may have
been composed in any century—the heart in them
as well as in me—a human heart, which cries
out for the living God, whatever our critical heart
cries out for—will accept it as a revelation ; we
shall cling to it and love it as we never can love any
books or any theories which are merely assented
to because we are told there is some superlative
evidence for them which we ought to acknowledge.
And then when once this Gospel of the Atonement,
of an actual Reconciler and a real Reconciliation,
has made itself heard above the din of explanations and controversies—if it be only in a few ears
—creeds and sacraments will come forth again as
the simple witnesses, to all creatures in all lands,

that the Prince of Darkness has been overcome,
that they are in the Kingdom of God.   At the
first Reformation the intense individual feeling of
those who received the good news marred the
effect of it as a testimony to the societies of men.
In us that social feeling must be addressed first,
the individual consciousness can only be reached
through it.   If there is no Atonement for us all,
there is no Atonement for any one of us.   There
may be theories of sacrifice without number:
the sacrifice must be for Man, or it is not for any
man.

The fanaticism which led many of the Reformers to cry out for the destruction of the
Mass was very excusable.   It seemed to them a
terrible mockery of all that was most sacred and
divine, a denial of the very blessing of which it
contained the sign and the promise.   But the
Mass has lasted to our day: it has not been
altered; it excites the same feeling of indignation
in many men as it did three centuries ago; but
it has also an immense, even an irresistible
attraction for many who have not been brought
up under the shadow of it, who were taught in
their infancy to abhor it.   Some say that it
speaks of something which might be believed in
former days: some feel that the oppressions of

the nineteenth century demand such a belief as
much as those of any century. We do want it
more than our forefathers did! We want the
belief of an actual atonement, not an imaginary
one. We cannot acknowledge, as some say that
they can, a kindly Father who leaves His children
to perish in their own wilfulness. We cannot
always be satisfied with talk about civilization and
the progress of the species. Does God civilize?
Does He care for the progress of the species or of
individuals? The people will ask this question.
It will arise out of their deepest heart. The
critics cannot answer it. Can the Devil? Can
He who, as we say, came to destoy the works of
the Devil? If He answers it, there will indeed
be a reformation. Prayers will not be disjoined
from sacrifice. The Son who said, " Lo, I came
to do Thy will, O God," is the High Priest of all
who say, " Thy will be done on earth as it is in
Heaven: " He who with strong cries and tears
prayed to Him that could deliver from death, is
the High Priest of all who say, " Deliver us
from evil."

And who can help forward this reformation
better than you, my friend? We debate about
the word propitiation. We ask ourselves what
St. Paul meant when he spoke of God setting

forth His Son as a propitiation through faith in
His blood, to declare His righteousness, for the re-
mission of sins that are past ?   Did he mean that
Jesus poured out His blood to buy off the wrath
of His Father?   We, I say, *debate* this question.
You can answer it.   You know what propitiations to Gods that want to be bought off—who
demand compensations for pardon—are.   You
know that the conception of the Unseen Power
in which these thoughts originated is the conception of an Evil Power, and that the fruits of that
conception are immoral, degrading, destructive.
You may have the utmost sympathy with those who
have fallen into such conceptions.   You may not
feel that you have the least right to condemn them,
knowing that you are tempted to the same.   But
it is from these conceptions—exactly from these
—that you go forth to rescue your fellow-men.
It is with these that you are carrying on an un-
compromising, exterminating warfare.   You have
learnt what the weapons of that warfare must
be.   You understand the deep inward yearning
that prompts the cry for propitiation.   You
believe that yearning to be divinely inspired, to
exist in men because they are created to know
God, and to be at peace with Him.   And therefore you cannot subvert propitiations to evil

powers, except by bringing out in its full force the propitiation which is prompted simply by the Divine Love, which is given without money and price, which is set forth in the Son who is the express image of the Father, whose sacrifice is the fulfilment of the Father's will. The two thoughts *correspond* to each other undoubtedly. The Devil's counterfeit must always correspond to the image which it mocks. But woe to you if that correspondence tempts you to put the one, or any modification of the one, for the other! Woe to you if, under pretence of meeting the heathen half way, or from a dim notion that you can cure his schemes of compensation by telling him of a larger and more adequate compensation, you establish all his worst thoughts, you ratify his homage to evil powers under new names! This, my friend, is your peril, as it has been the peril of Christendom in all its missionary enterprises. Resist it in God's strength, and so bring *us* back to the faith of God's elect, to that real communion with sufferers on earth and spirits about the Throne, of which the Mass has presented the feeblest of all likenesses, but the hope of which it may through God's gracious providence have kept alive in many hearts.—Yours, &c.

LETTER XI.

THE CHURCH OF THE ETERNAL.

My DEAR FRIEND,—When the Bishop of Oxford spoke of our indifference to theological doctrines and theological distinctions, he was probably thinking especially of the doctrine of the Atonement, and of the distinction of Persons in the Holy Trinity. On the former subject I spoke in my last letter. Our indifference to the meaning of Atonement and Sacrifice, as it is set forth in that book of the New Testament which is expressly devoted to the treatment of them, —our disposition to substitute for this meaning or to blend with it one which is essentially contrary to it,—this, it seemed to me, was leading us rapidly to that confusion between the God in Whom is light and no darkness, and the Prince of Darkness, which the Bishop said was threatening us. In this letter I turn to the other still more awful, still more radical

12

principle of theology—that which is expressed in
the form of our Baptism, which is the ground-
work of the Creeds.

"God," said St. Paul to the inhabitants of
the city which was wholly given to idolatry, to
men who were mocking him and calling him a
babbler—"*God is not far from any one of us, for
in Him we live, and move, and have our being.*"
Who was this God of whom he speaks ?   We
say, " The Father of an infinite majesty ; His
honourable, true, and only Son ; also the Holy
Ghost the Comforter."   This is the One God,
blessed for ever, in Whom we live, and move, and
have our being.   We are baptized into this
Name ; we bring our children to be baptized
into it.   We pronounce it after every Psalm
which was written in the old time : we declare
that this Name was in the beginning, is now, and
ever shall be, world without end.   We invoke
this Name when we are praying against pride,
malice, and uncharitableness ; against fornication
and all deadly sin ; against plague, pestilence and
famine, battle, murder and sudden death ; against
heresy, schism and contempt of the divine
words and commandments.   In this Name we
bless our congregations : to know this Name,
we tell them, is the glory of the saints about

the Throne. Eternal salvation is connected in
the Athanasian Creed with this Name, eternal
damnation with the loss of it.

Our Church then, by its initial rites, by
its forms of worship, by its solemnest professions of faith, affirms that it stands in this
Name. So far as it is a Missionary Church,
it aspires to seal the nations with this Name.
That is its commission; it can plead no other
right to go forth on any errand of conversion.
And its course with reference to the nations
is clearly defined. If we recognize St. Paul as
the great missionary, we can have no doubt
about it. We tell all men, those who are most
incredulous of our message, most hostile to it,
that this Name is about them, that they are
living, moving, having their being in it. They
do not acquire this privilege by baptism: we
baptize them because they have it.

Now is it not true that the greatest theological indistinctness prevails on this subject, not
among those who profess to disbelieve the Trinity
only, but among those who make the most vehement profession of acknowledging the Trinity?
Do we affirm that this Name indeed compasses the
universe, that it is not far from any one of us?
Do we not say that Arians, Unitarians, Sabellians,

and a multitude who partly share their tenets without knowing it, are outside this Name—that they have no part or lot in it ? Do we not question whether Quakers can have much to do with it, since they refuse the outward sign and pledge of being adopted into it ? Do we not therefore say *à fortiori* that men of the kind whom St. Paul addressed on Mars' Hill are altogether aloof from it ?

Here is a difference between our theology and that of the Apostles who were sent forth to baptize the nations—between our theology and the theology of our services and sacraments—which cannot long be hidden, which must stand out glaringly in our practice. Many circumstances in our time, those especially to which the Bishop alludes, compel us to notice and reflect upon it. There is, he hints, a disposition to fraternize on the ground of indifference or unbelief. ' We ' cannot know much,' is the cry of many, ' about ' the heavenly or unseen world ; if there are ' truths concerning it, they do not concern us. ' Let us meet on the broad basis of our earthly ' interests, or of acts of service to our fellow- ' creatures. Theology may go where it will.' Well ! this scheme is not only announced ; it is acted out by strong churchmen, by preachers, and

divines of the High Church and the Low Church
schools. They meet the Unitarians and Quakers
whom they excommunicate on the ground of
earthly interests : they will buy of either, or sell
to either. They meet both when they are devising
sanitary measures for the good of cities, or benevolent measures for employing, if not educating,
the poor. Think what an effect this indifference
to theology, this acknowledgment that a broader
basis than that which it affords, may be found in
the ordinary conditions of daily life, must have
when it is seen in those who in their schools
and synods treat theology as the most important
subject of all, the bond between heaven and earth !
Have not men who avow infidelity a right to say,
" Whatever you may pretend, theology is that
which separates you into little circles. You
never break loose from those circles, you never
take up your position as men among men except
when you forget it." That such words are
spoken continually, that such facts afford a
justification for them, we do not want a Bishop
to inform us. But no one is more capable of
awakening us to the significancy of the words
—he is never more entirely fulfilling his office
than when he leads us to reflect on the preg-
nancy of the facts.

Will he then go on to urge that excommunication in its old sense should be revived— that the intercourse of society, the buying and selling in shops, should be made dependent on theological opinions? That remedy for the evil may be suggested: if it is adopted it must be adopted thoroughly. No half measures can be of the least avail: every concession is the concession of a principle, practically of the whole principle which is at issue. The Bishop did not propose a recurrence to a course which he knew to be impossible. He took the far wiser method of urging us seriously to consider what we do believe, of conjuring us not to let *that* go.

Here, indeed, is a remedy. If I consider what I say that I believe, if I determine to hold that fast, I may discover that I have in theology a much broader as well as firmer meeting-ground with men as men, with men of all kinds and professions, of all modes and habits of thought, with men who attack my convictions, with men who are indifferent about their own convictions, than any maxims of trade, of convenience, of modern civilization, of modern tolerance, can supply me with. I may find how it is that the most practical and energetic of those maxims

have been developed and are able to exercise
so much power in the world ; what it is that has
enfeebled them and made them an excuse for
insincere evasions, for a sham politeness covering
an inward dislike.   If I believed in the Trinity—
if I accepted the form of my baptism, interpreted
by the Apostle of the Gentiles, as the expression
of an actual truth—I must have a bond of union
with Arians, Unitarians, Sabellians, as well as
with those who reject the form of baptism, which
I certainly could never obtain through the necessity of bargaining with them or sitting with them
at dinner-parties.   I must believe that the God
whom I worship is not far from any one of them,
that they are in His presence at every moment,
that the love of the Father, the Son, and the
Spirit is an atmosphere which is surrounding
them as much as it is surrounding me, that I
have no right to dwell in it which is not also
their right.   I cannot make the acts of the
Father or the Son dependent on their confession
of the Father and the Son.   What would become
of me if those acts were dependent on *my* confession of them !   I cannot measure the power
of the Spirit over them by their recognition of
His power ; if I did I should not be able to account
for any of the good thoughts and deeds which

must, according to my creed, flow from that
Spirit—which can have no other source. Whatever recognition there is in them of any Person in
the Trinity I must, if I hold fast my faith,
attribute to the influence of the Trinity upon
them; whatever denial there is of any Person in
the Trinity, I know that I cannot remove by any
arguments of mine. If it is overcome, the Spirit
of truth must overcome it. I shall be His
minister in overcoming it so far as I am governed
by Him; if I am resisting Him or letting another
spirit—the contentious, dividing, persecuting
spirit—usurp his throne in me, I shall confirm
the denial.

"All this is very well," I shall be told; "it
is true in a certain sense. Of course we ought to
deal charitably with opponents; but we must
maintain the truth once delivered to the saints."
Just so; it is what I am saying—further that we
must not let any sense, certain or uncertain, interfere with this duty; that our allegiance to the faith
once delivered to the saints demands it of us;
that we are traitors to that faith whenever we do
not perform it. How much of such treachery
there has been in me, how little I understand
that human fellowship of which I speak, how
awkward I often feel in the company of those

who dissent from the convictions which I hold
dear, how inclined I am to treat them as incapable
of entering into any deep truth, how readily I
assume that we can only converse about the
weather or the stocks—this I must sadly and
shamefully confess. But I know that the spirit
which prompts this kind of feeling is the spirit of
vanity, of dogmatism, of heresy, not the Spirit
of the Father and the Son. I know that if I
were thoroughly possessed and penetrated by that
Spirit, I should find myself in sympathy with the
beliefs of all sorts of men, that I should hate
their denials and my own, and should be always
enlisting their beliefs against their denials. Till
I do this, I shall not count that I am making a
true confession of my faith in the Holy Trinity.
I shall always suspect that I am confounding the
Persons or dividing the Substance.

This language about Persons and Substance,
which is to me most real, which speaks to my conscience and detects my moral obliquities, conveys
no sense whatever to many minds. Is it not mad-
ness in me, and wild fighting against God, to
insist that it should convey a sense to them? If
I am thankful to God for preserving that and every
other form of speech which has a true scientific
force, for the use of mankind, I may be equally

thankful to Him that He leads His children by
the most different routes to the knowledge of
Him. I may be thankful that no ignorance of
metaphysics and no bad metaphysics can hinder
the operation of His Spirit, the revelation of His
truth. If the message of the gospel, the words
of Christ's commission, have not deceived us,
the operation of that Spirit, the revelation of that
Truth, must be for the commonest people of the
earth, for all nations.

And where is the church which is entrusted
with this gospel and commission? Suppose I
were to say, " It is the Church of England, *not*
the Church of Italy, *not* the Church of France, *not*
the Church of Russia," should I not be denying
the baptismal formula, should I not be excluding
those who are marked out by a simple and comprehensive sign for a mighty work? Whatever
church does say this, surely disclaims its own
title-deeds, refuses to assert its office, makes itself
heretical. How ready *every* church is to make
itself heretical by separating itself from the rest,
how ready it is to fraternise in some opinions, and
so to deny the Head of the whole body, I have
already confessed. It is the sin for which we have
all to seek repentance; it is the homage to the
Evil Spirit, the Spirit of Antichrist, which we have

all paid. We have accused each other of being
heretics, and we have all been heretics. We have
all set up notions and dogmas of our under-
standings against Him who has given us under-
standings, against Him who is guiding us to seek
for that Truth which passes all our under-
standings. We have said that there is such a
Truth, that in it we have eternal life. And
then we reduce this too down to the level of our
conceptions. What *we* hold about the Name
which we declare in the most solemn language
to be incomprehensible and eternal, is substituted for the Name ; we believe in ourselves—
in what we think—not in God.

But such a belief as this cannot last ; our notions
will not uphold us when we are sinking in deep
waters. We may call in evidences, arguments,
authority, what we will ; but if they are not GOD,
they will not help creatures who are made in the
likeness of God, who demand Him as the object
of their trust. If we do not worship Him, we
shall worship the Spirit that is opposed to Him:
we shall pay sacrifice to the Author of eternal
death, because the Author of eternal life is
banished from us.

We, then, who repeat the Athanasian Creed
may have much need to reflect upon what we call

its damnatory clauses. They may have a far
more awful sense than we have seen in them.
They may say to us, " *You* may put yourselves
out of fellowship with the Spirit of truth and
love. *You* may bid the Holy One cease from
before you." Wherever else *Eternal* death is
taken to mean *future* death, it cannot be so taken
in this creed, unless its own most serious words
are emptied of their significance. The word
eternal has been expressly associated with Him
who is, and was, and is to come ; if it occurs
in a later passage of the same document, that
sense must be given to it there. The eternal
life must be the life of the Eternal God of which
men are permitted to partake. The eternal death
must be the separation from the Eternal God,
whatever may be the length of that separation.
Let those who insist upon the natural sense
of theological expressions see to it that they
adhere to the natural sense of this expression in
the creed to which they appeal most. Let
them then consider what havoc they make of
the divinest promises and threatenings of the New
Testament, if they introduce any other sense into
its inspired language.

Oh, my friend ! it is not to weaken the
strength of these promises and threatenings,

that I have written to you.   They overwhelm me
with their grandeur and their terror.   I believe
that God is arousing us to feel that grandeur and
that terror as we have never felt it.   The loss
of the God of infinite charity, the exclusion from
fellowship with Him, what plummets of ours can
measure this abyss?   And are we not in danger
of it every hour?   Is not the danger greatest
when our security is greatest?   If we abide in
opinions—any opinions whatsoever—the hurri-
cane will sweep our refuges away, they will prove
to be refuges of lies.   If we abide in the Father
and the Son, we must be safe.   But the Son
said—and He spoke the mind of His father—
" *Judge not, that you be not judged.   For with
what judgment you judge, you shall be judged, and
with what measure you mete, it shall be measured to
you again.*"   And that same Son said, " *If you
that are fathers give good gifts to your children, shall
not my Father in heaven give the Holy Spirit to
them that ask Him?* "   We may in the full sense
of our unholiness, untruthfulness, unloveliness,
ask for the Spirit of Holiness, of Truth and
Love.   He can expel from us the spirit which
leads us into impurity, hatred, and falsehood.

When that Holy Spirit indeed fills the church,
its proper dwelling-place, what shall that church

be called ? We hear much of the Church of the *Past*. The Apostolic age, the age of the Fathers, the Middle age, have each their champions. To recover the traditions of other times, is said to be the great duty of our time. We have many who are equally opposed to these retrospections, to the novelties which are imported from foreign lands, to the dreams of individual projectors. They cling to the Church *of the Present*. There are of course many divisions of that church. The conservative defends that division of it with which he has local and hereditary sympathies : the others, in proportion as they differ from that, he suspects of not having any part or lot in the divine body. Not a few ardent spirits, and some by no means ardent, have pictured to themselves a Church *of the Future*. The pictures are inevitably unlike : one may be highly coloured, one may be conspicuous only for its neutral tint. But all foretell that this church shall be a contrast to what we see around us, or read of in history.

The church which I am occupied with, cannot answer to any of these names. Yet it may do, it must do, justice to the thoughts which each represents. It cannot shut itself up in the habits and modes of thinking of any

period. It is by its profession the CHURCH OF
THE ETERNAL, of Him who is, and who was, and
who is to come. If it abandons this profession,
it ceases to shine with any divine glory : its glory
is its own.

I know that when one speaks, though it be
in the language of St. Paul and St. John, of
" dwelling in God," of " abiding in the Father
and the Son," a suspicion immediately arises that
Pantheism is creeping in. Distinguished men of
the rationalist school have said that the Apostle
of the Gentiles when he wrote to the Ephesians
of " one God and Father of all, who is above all,
and through all, and in you all," was anticipating
Spinoza. And so perhaps he would have been,
if he had not written in the same Epistle—" We
wrestle not with flesh and blood, but with prin-
cipalities and powers, with the rulers of the darkness of this world, with spiritual wickedness in
high places." If the Apostle had not been a
fighter, if he had not confessed at every moment
a deadly adversary of himself and of his kind, he
might have plunged into that gulf in which it has
been said that all moral, as well as all theological,
distinctions are lost. Men who have not the
sense of a war in themselves and in the universe,
in which Good or Evil—a SPIRIT of good or of

evil—must triumph at last, may find just as much
Pantheism in the excommunicated Jew of Tarsus
as in the excommunicated Jew of Amsterdam.　If
they do not, I must reckon it a proof that they
have entered far less into the mind of the Apostle
than his countryman did.　On the other hand
those who *are* engaged in such a struggle may
have the intensest sympathy with that profound
perception of the necessity of God to their own
existence,—of the impossibility of living and
moving without God—which was imparted to
Spinoza.　They will not doubt that the God
of his fathers gave him that perception.　But
they will find a depth below his depth, in the
Psalmist, who fled to God as a refuge from his
enemies, who cried to God, " Why hast Thou
forsaken me ? "　They will have an affection for
Spinoza which those who go to him for arguments
against the reality of his nation's history cannot
have.　They will never charge it as a crime upon a
man in his circumstances—cut off from one people,
not naturalized in another—that he was unable
to perceive the simplicity and continuousness of
that history.　They will rejoice that they are not
obliged to sink Humanity in Divinity as he was ;
that they can acknowledge One who is perfect
God and perfect Man.　They will reflect how he

may rise in judgment against them for confessing
Jesus to be the image of the Father, and yet not
yielding to that love which Spinoza felt in his
inspired moments—whatever the critics who reverence him only for being unlike vulgar people
may say to the contrary—was embracing and
penetrating the universe.

To deny that doctrine may be to escape from
Spinoza ; it is not to follow St. Paul.   As his
Master had endured the contradiction of Pharisees
because He would preach the kingdom of God to
publicans and harlots, and invite them to enter
it, so St. Paul declared that the offence of the
Cross would cease if he were willing to preach
circumcision, to adopt the exclusiveness of his
race, to deny that the Head of every man had
appeared.   And now we are commanded in the
name of Paul, in the name of Jesus, to make
the universal Church as narrow as we can,
because the Sermon on the Mount has declared
that " strait is the gate, and narrow is the way
which leadeth to life, and few there be that find
it."   What true and wonderful words those are !
How beautifully they are illustrated by the context
of that discourse which bids us be like our Father
in Heaven, who sends His rain on the just and
the unjust, the good and the evil; which sets

13

forth everywhere the contrast between His mind and that of the Pharisees. "Strait indeed is the gate," since any man who would enter it must stoop low down to the level of the meanest of the race! "Narrow indeed is the way," for he who has passed through the gate must not then lift himself as if he had become different from others through that humiliation! It must continue through his whole pilgrimage: he must be every day learning more and more how disposed he is to exalt himself on his wisdom or his righteousness, on his faith or his works; he must be discovering the vanity and falsehood of that boast; he must be brought down to the state of the child and the beggar. A narrow way indeed! if that is the way to life, which of us can find it? Surely not one, if God did not Himself, by severe discipline, draw him out of that broad way into which all men are disposed to run, the way of thinking himself good and right and despising others. The eternal life, —the life of the Eternal God—can never surely be reached by any of us till we see Him as Christ revealed Him to us, till we understand what He is through the Death for all men which was the perfect fulfilment of His will, the perfect satisfaction of His love,—till therefore we re-

nounce all exclusiveness, till we confess a charity
which is surrounding us all and seeking to bring
us all within its circle.

"What, then, would you include Jews, Turks,
infidels, heretics of all kinds, within your Church
of the Eternal?" I would include none within
it who would not include themselves. The
Romish scheme of compelling people to come
in has been tried long enough, and has not suc-
ceeded so well that one would wish to revive it.
But supposing there is such a Church as this, supposing any of us may claim a portion in it, the
reason must be that we confess God is drawing us
into it, and that this drawing of His has a com-
pulsion in it which, however long it may be
resisted, will prevail at last over the stubbornest
wills. If we consider that we have not stubborn
wills, or that we have less stubborn wills than
those who have had fewer blessings, I hope we
shall be converted from that opinion; while we
hold it, how can we walk in the way that leadeth
to life, how can we confess our sins or humble
ourselves before God? Do we fear the reproach
of saying that the Love, the everlasting, unchang-
ing Love, of God, is about Jews, Turks, infidels,
and heretics? Then let us preach no Gospel,
let us send forth no missionaries, let us not

13—2

repeat our Good Friday prayer. That Prayer must be a falsehood on our lips, unless we believe that the Love of Calvary is what St. Paul affirmed it to be.

My friend, it is and will be the offence of the cross in our day to make this confession in defiance, not of circumcised, but of baptized men. In doing it we shall glorify our baptism as no exclusiveness can glorify it,—for we shall glorify the Holy Trinity. Against the notion of being required to adopt a formula, to accept theological refinements, the age rebels, and will rebel more and more. Instead of complaining that it is so, let us believe that God has Himself inspired the rebellion that He may teach us not to believe in a formula, but in the Being of whom the formula speaks. What greater mercy can He show us than this ? What is more terrible than to say : We believe in the Father, and not to draw nigh to Him as if He were the Father ; We believe in the Son, and only to think of Him as shut up in the leaves of a book ; We believe in the Holy Ghost, and never to own when He convinces us of sin, of righteousness, of judgment ; never to be guided by Him into love and truth ? O God ! shatter our formulas as thy servant of old brake in pieces the brazen serpent, rather than that they should lead us to such perdition as this! But, oh! by them or without them, by us or without us, let thy reconciling Name be revealed to the sons of men, to Jews, Turks, heathens, and to us heretics of all kinds and schools, that we may be one even as Thou, Father, art in the Son, and the Son is in Thee, united in the blessed Spirit of peace and holiness for ever.— Yours, &c.

LETTER XII.

CHRISTIANITY AND CIVILIZATION.

MY DEAR FRIEND,—You are often told. by philo-
sophical friends at home that a missionary must
seek to civilize before he seeks to convert. You
are often warned by theological friends that your
first duty is to teach Christianity; many of the
fruits of civilization will no doubt follow when
that has been faithfully received.

A long controversy; to you sometimes a dis-
tracting one—oftener, I should suppose, a weari-
some one. While you deal with these phrases,
Christianity and Civilization, it must be an end-
less one. Each requires translation, and who is
to be the translator? Christianity, if it is taken
as the complex of notions and habits which
belong to Christendom, to the countries which
acknowledge Jesus as the Christ, may be treated
as one of the phenomena of modern civilization.
Somehow men in this Western world have been

brought to adopt these notions and habits; they have undergone various alterations and transformations; they have been partly inherited, partly acquired ; they have still a great influence on society.   But when. you proceed to examine this phenomenon further, you are met with most tormenting questions as to the number of these notions and habits which belong to Christianity, or to something quite different from Christianity.   You hear most various answers to these questions from those who profess a general agreement with each other, who are citizens of the same nation, who are even united in the same sect or school.

If you look at the subject from the other side, you encounter equal difficulties.   You are to impart civilization.   What civilization ?   Is the East to receive all the customs and practices which the West consecrates with that name ?   Are you so satisfied with the civilization of France, or Italy, or England, that you would transfer that whole to India or China, suppose it were in your power to do so, suppose you were not brought face to face with another kind of civilization which treats yours as barbarism ?

These are—you know it well—practical, not speculative difficulties.   The practical Englishman indeed cuts through them: he has a strong rough faith that what he holds, it must be good for every man to hold, that what he is it would be good for every man to be. It is, I say, a *faith* of a real kind so far as it goes; perhaps there is a deeper faith in it than the person who exercises it is quite aware of: it is not only or chiefly a faith in what an individual can accomplish, it is an assurance that he is one of a race which has a calling to vanquish and renovate. Therefore it has had, and still has, an amazing success, but a success which we are sometimes reminded has a limit, which has turned and may turn to great discomfiture. And if the civilization at home should prove to be weak—weak in its very roots—if there should be a discovery that its blessings only reach a small minority of those who dwell in the land which boasts of it most, and that within this minority there is much which is not sound, which is even rotten, what becomes of the attempt to diffuse this civilization? Who will make the attempt? What will the attempt be good for?

Such considerations may be easily banished from our minds by agreeable self-flatteries mixed with some earnest truths. But they cannot easily be banished from your mind; you must

work out this problem, you must find some way
of solving it.

The hint which I have given you is so simple
and obvious a one that you may be inclined to
pass it by. But perhaps it deserves consideration. *We* have connected Christianity with the
Name into which we are baptized. It does not
signify to us what other men think. They may
have a different conception of the whole subject.
Unitarians may laugh immensely at the credulity
which binds us to an old superstition, or may
charge us solemnly with denying the unity of
God. We cannot blame them for doing so ; but
we must blame ourselves if we make a profession
by our creeds, to which we afterwards attach no
importance in our acts. We have declared that
not some notions or habits of ours were the
objects of our faith, or the grounds of our faith :
that in the Father, the Son, and the Spirit, the
one God blessed for ever, we have both the
ground and object of it. This has been, and is,
our confession : this has been and is the definition
and warrant of your enterprise. How does it
apply to the question as to the relation between
Christianity and Civilization ?

The whole dispute as to the different kinds
and forms of Christianity, as to the different

opinions which do or do not enter, or should or
should not enter, into the scheme of Christianity
—the very word, as having no authority in Scripture, no place in the creeds—you may dismiss
at once. And in declining to decide between
the disputants, you take up no new ground : you
simply stand on the old ground; you refuse to
abandon that which Christendom has recognized,
in terms, as the bond of its fellowship; you
refuse to substitute heresies, Roman, Greek,
Anglican, for the Church of God.

Then as to the other demand, or rather the
two demands, Ought not you to civilize, and if
to civilize, then what is to be the shape and
mould of your civilization ? To the first you
answer, I believe in a Spirit who is at work on
the inner life of human society, who is contending with all that makes it brutal or effeminate,
slavish or anarchical. I believe in a Spirit who
is not content with the semblances of civility
and manliness, of freedom or order, who seeks to
deliver us from whatever makes us ungracious
to each other, cowardly in our resolutions and
acts, from whatever leads us to crouch to any
tyrant, or to set up any form of self-will in
our own hearts. I believe in a Spirit who can
never be satisfied till He awakens real energies :

till those energies bring forth fruit in action. I
believe in a Spirit who carries on continuously a
conflict with the sloth and feebleness in me and in
my fellow-creatures : who will give them and me
no rest till He casts out from us the devils of
sloth and feebleness. This Spirit I am to
proclaim wherever I go. I am to say that He
is the Spirit of the Father who has created us
in His Son, of the Son who has redeemed us as
His brethren. I am to assure those who hear
me that their baptism means that they may be
possessed by this civilizing, reconciling, uniting
Spirit, that they need not be possessed by any
other; though the struggle between them will
always be fierce—more, not less fierce, when they
have claimed their place in the universal family,
than when they have supposed themselves separate creatures, the servants of demons, the
victims of malignant powers which they must
propitiate.

And surely we then dispose of the other
question, " *What* civilization will you bestow on
these men ? " You cannot mould them, thank
God ! into English or European fashions; you
cannot subvert or alter any part of the Oriental
constitution which He has seen fit that they
should possess. We have learnt the best

wisdom which books can impart out of an
Oriental book : that has given us our lessons in
what is human, what is universal : that has been
a continued protest against the exclusiveness of
our Western habits. What is dark, unwhole-
some, dividing, in Oriental manners, the Spirit
of holiness and truth will strive against ; what
is graceful, generous, sincere in them, He will
bring forth in its might ; these will be our
examples and warnings, these He will not allow
any coarse or restless tempers of our continent
to displace.

This will be your mode of dealing with this
embarrassing question, on which so much of the
modern learning about races has been thrown
away. Such learning may be exceedingly useful
in pointing out the different aspects under which
the same truth may present itself to different kinds
of men, very useful in showing how the divine
education has been working in one or another part
of the world. It becomes mischievous when it is
used to prove that there is no common truth which
may embrace all human beings, no divine education which may lead them into that truth. That
this lore respecting races, grounded on physio-
logical observations and political experience, has
been pleaded as the justification of slavery—that

doctrines of equality loudly asserted, and a scheme of society apparently based upon them, could not overcome that justification—that a great war has been the only answer to it —this the most recent facts proclaim to us. Would that war have been necessary if the Church—instead of regarding itself as an artificial Society, either opposed to states and nations, more exclusive than any, or else as bound to accept and endorse the habits of any nation in which it was tolerated—had proclaimed all men of every race and colour to be sons of God in Christ the Son of Man, and had recognized at the same time all differences of habits, temperaments, mental or physical constitution, which· have been manifested in fact or detected by science, as signs of the need of a culture which only a Divine Spirit who knows the conditions of every man and every society can give us wisdom to impart or can make effectual?

I need not tell you that such language will sound particularly offensive to those who speak most in our day of civilization. If they recognize some modification of Christianity as beneficial to the world in its present state, it would be especially *such* a modification as would exclude all idea of a Good Spirit or an Evil Spirit. If they recognize a certain improvement in the tone of Christians — something which indicates an advance upon the notions of the early age, or the middle age, or the age of the Reformers—the improvement is this—that while we adopt the dialect of our predecessors respecting a Divine Teacher and a holy or unholy inspiration, we do not, in fact, believe in them, but treat any genuine believer in them as fanatical. This appears to the worshippers of Civilization a step in the right direction. They are puzzled, indeed, by two observations. The first is, that the more unbelieving we have become respecting these inward illuminations, the more we are offended by any questions which have been raised about the books of Scripture. The second is, that on the very summit of Civilization—in the select, even the scientific circles which represent it—there has appeared, even in the most grotesque and superstitious shape, a *demand* for spiritual communication, for intercourse with the invisible world, *of some kind.* So that the gain on our part seems at least questionable, the security on theirs against the enthusiasm which has deserted us, very precarious indeed.

Therefore, those bolder men who affirm that

Christianity now as well as in older days—
now more than in older days—is, under every
form which it may assume, a hindrance to civilization, are far more likely to obtain credence
than these compromisers. They can appeal
with mighty force to our divisions and animo-
sities; they can prove that these augment and
exasperate, if they do not produce, all the strifes
which are at work in nations and families;
they can ask whether such a nuisance must not
be abated, if the world is to be reformed. I
think so; I hope you think so. If you believe
in the Spirit of unity, the Spirit of the Father
and the Son, you must think so. And, if you do,
you must also believe that that which civilization
cannot effect through the weakness of the flesh
by any of its arts, will be effected by the mighty
energy of the power which it has denied; that
the abuses which it can only sweep away by
destroying itself, will be swept away by Him who
can make — who is continually making — all
things new. Let, then, these denouncers of our
Christianity raise their voices to the loudest pitch.
They may bring home to our consciences the
guilt of Devil-worship, though they say there is
no Devil. They may show us that we have been
traitors to the Spirit of truth and love, though

they may call us madmen for confessing such a Spirit.

And if they do lead us to confession and repentance, there will be the dawn for the world of a brighter and nobler civilization than any which they have dreamed of. A civilization without a Spirit is a civilization which must always be limited to the easy and comfortable portion of society. It will affect their behaviour, not their manners; it will come forth in an external and dishonest politeness, not in gentleness and grace. In a commerical community, the possession of money will be the highest sign of it. Art, literature, science, religion will bow to that, and will take its standard for their standard. The mass of the people will be regarded as dangerous. To keep them from mischief—if preaching does not avail—they may be offered education, or amusement, or a share of political power. But they will not be reverenced as men; for that is not the distinction upon which their superiors value themselves—rather upon their being unlike the rest of mankind.

The poor of the earth have always craved for this message of a Divine Spirit, have always felt, however they may have expressed the feeling, that some Spirit, not divine, but the contrary of divine, was oppressing and tormenting them. Civilization tells them they are deluded in these convictions; but civilization does not happen to know what is going on in their hovels or in their hearts. Whenever a gospel penetrates into them we may hear strange things. The son of a Saxon miner— an English tinker—may have deadly conflicts with the Devil, by the reports of which witty men will be greatly amused. But the miner's son comes forth from his battle to emancipate the Nations; the tinker rises from a barbarian into a cultivated man capable of writing a *Pilgrim's Progress*, capable of speaking to the spirits of multitudes in his own class and in all classes; recognized by them as a fellow sufferer and a fellow man, even when his formal language seems most to exclude them from that privilege or to assert another for himself.

Was he wrong, or was Luther wrong, in that which was the central thought of their lives? Wrong I should say so far as either of them supposed that he was not wrestling with a Spirit, but with a visible shape; wrong so far as either of them believed that their conflicts were different in kind from those of human creatures in all places and times. Right so far as they held and taught what facts proclaim abroad to all who will hear them, what facts proclaim in our own selves

14

if we do not prefer dreams to facts,—that there is something (if you call it a *body*, then you fall into the error which we impute to Luther and Bunyan—I call it a *Spirit* that I may avoid their error,) which draws us to be enemies of each other, enemies of Peace, of Justice, of Truth. A conviction which would be absolutely intolerable if it were not met and overreached by another,— that this Spirit is withdrawing us from the control of that Spirit who has been the spring of all the beauty and harmony that appears in God's outward creation, or in man His image.

My Friend! it is a hard fight to believe that this Spirit is the stronger, not the weaker of the two. You know how hard it is. But it is the very fight of faith. We cease to believe at all when we cease to believe this. Nothing drives us to it like despair of ourselves, like the certainty that we must sink to an ever lower death, if there is not One who would raise us to the highest life. Out of that despair springs a hope for all. No spirit can be out of the reach of God's Spirit. No part of creation can be beyond the government of Him who has subdued human hearts, who has the keys of death and hell. A Father who can own us as His children, who can enable us in spite of our reluctance and obstinacy to

claim the title, will not yield at last to the
father of lies. It may seem to us, sometimes, as
if death had vanquished life in this world. But
the earth comes fresh each morning out of the
darkness in which she had been buried. It
seems at times as if division were to banish
peace for ever. But there is forgiveness among
enemies, reconciliation of friends; the wars of
nations end at last. It seems at times as if the
God of Damnation was hiding the God of Salvation from the sight of us and of all men. But
no unbelief of ours can subvert the faith of
God. By the promise of a new heaven and a
new earth, some understand another heaven and
another earth. Would that be a promise?—
that .there should be another heaven than that
in which God dwells, another earth than that
which He pronounced very good? No, surely.
Christ proclaimed the new heaven when he said,
Go into all the nations, which have had a heaven
of dark demons, or of a mere arbitrary Sovereign, and baptize them in the all-loving Name.
The earth was declared to be a new earth
when the Son walked upon it, and died in it,
and rose in it, when the Spirit took possession of poor men's hearts and lips, and bound
them into a human family. It will be indeed a

new heaven when all the evil thoughts which we have cherished about God shall yield to the full revelation of Himself. It will be a new earth when all that has defiled its beauty, all that has filled it with death and misery, shall be purged away. If it is the privilege of the spirits of just men made perfect to know the reality of that heaven which they believed in here; to see the earth which they beheld here, as God sees it—we may enter into their blessedness so far as we relinquish all thought of a heaven or an earth made for our selfish pleasure, so far as we desire a heaven and an earth in which the glory of God shall be unveiled to all the creatures whom He has made. —Yours, &c.

THE END.

London: Printed by SMITH, ELDER AND Co., Old Bailey, E.C.

BV - #0020 - 110723 - C0 - 229/152/13 - PB - 9781527687288 - Gloss Lamination